P9-DGE-499

THE ULTIMATE STRANGER

CARL H. DELACATO, ED.D.

THE
ULTIMATE
STRANGER
The Autistic Child

Doubleday & Company, Inc., Garden City, New York, 1974

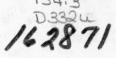

This Book Is Gratefully Dedicated to
L.C.B., A.S.E., and N.A.F.
For all that they have done for children

FOREWORD

This book describes a personal journey into a strange and alien world—the world of the autistic child. Autistic children have been abandoned by all but a few. These lonely children, with their grotesque and alien behavior, are generally considered hopeless. Residential institutional placement is their usual final destination.

Early in my journey into the world of autism I found no familiar landmarks. I met no familiar names or faces. I met only the blank stares and the vacant faces of frightened children. They did not speak. They did not listen. And if I moved closer to them, they screamed in terror. Early in my journey I dubbed these alien children "the ultimate strangers."

At first I was guided by their mothers, as though I were blind. They allowed me to peek through the heavy curtain of despair surrounding their children. I began to learn a few primitive symbols of their language, the ancient and instinctive language of behavior. As I learned more, I found that the language was not primitive but was, instead, an emotion-laden cry for help.

I learned that I was the alien. I was the stranger, for I would not, I could not help.

As my journey progressed, I learned more of their hidden language. I ceased to be a threat to the children. They gradually allowed me to enter their world of fear. Often we were fearful together. But, as we learned from each other, our trust grew.

By midjourney they were no longer strangers, nor was I. They allowed me to listen to their calls for help. What had seemed, at the beginning of my journey, grotesque and alien behavior, had become a beautiful ballet with the child performing as both orchestra and dancer. He is also the composer and choreographer. Through a symphony of movement, he desperately attempts to make his autistic message understood. It is the ultimate creative act, the desperate cry of one human being to another—a cry for help.

This book tells what I learned during my journey. Whenever I write a book I, and those who work with me, am criticized. Five of my books deal with the learning process, a seemingly innocuous subject. But don't be fooled.

Each of those books has upset a section of the establishment. They have been criticized because they were addressed to both parents and professionals. Some of the critics claimed that the books created "false hope" for the parents. They were criticized because their main message was that the human brain could be changed through proper stimulation. Those books were invasions into new fields, and as a result I became not only the new competition, I was also a trespasser. These critics placed me in a position of being an invader or trespasser into an already staked-out territory.

But this book will be an exception. Since these hopeless and abandoned autistic children represent no establishment's territory, this book cannot be considered an invasion.

It does not trespass, for there are no "keep off" signs or fences in this territory. Indeed, this territory is a virtual desert. I encountered few footprints in the barren, lonely sands of my journey.

I journeyed alone. Along the way I was guided by some. If I have misused their advice, I alone am to blame, and I apologize. If there is to be criticism of my theory, I alone must bear the burden, for I alone am responsible.

I have chosen to leave The Institutes for the Achievement of Human Potential and plan to spend all my time journeying with those mothers and their autistic children.

To those courageous mothers and their beautiful children, who showed me the way, I shall always be grateful.

Carl H. Delacato
Thomas Road, Chestnut Hill
Philadelphia

CONTENTS

THE ULTIMATE STRANGER

I
AN ALIEN WORLD

Watching a child endlessly biting his own hand, or hypnotically spinning an ashtray, or blankly staring at a piece of dust for hours, or screaming like a wounded animal when you approach, or endlessly slapping his own face, or finger-painting his body with his own feces—all the while staring right through you—is frightening.

This is the autistic child. He ignores you, he is repulsed by human contact. He won't listen or talk to you, or allow you to touch him. He won't even look at another human being. His only pleasure, his only gratification, seems to come from his grotesque, repetitive, and often self-mutilative activity. He prefers things to people. He is always alone, locked up inside himself.

He is an alien in our midst. He almost seems possessed by some nonhuman power that compels him to carry out his own alien acts of self-destruction.

He is the ultimate stranger.

Because he is the ultimate stranger and alien to us, he is removed from our sight. He is labeled psychotic and is hidden in mental institutions.

More than six hundred thousand of these lonely aliens have been institutionalized for life, ostensibly because they are frightened by us, but, in truth, because they are frightening to us. Their alien behavior is incomprehensible and, therefore, frightening. Staring up at the windows of these institutions, you wonder how many mothers of those children will cry themselves to sleep tonight.

Another even more disturbing question gnaws at you. Is it possible that this *alien* behavior contains a hidden significance—a message to which we are blind? Is it possible that these children are desperately trying to communicate with us, and that we are deaf?

Is it possible that the biting, the spinning, the screaming, the slapping, even the painting of the body with his own feces, are all part of a code that we have, as yet, not broken?

Is it possible that the autistic child is desperately trying to communicate with us, and that we won't answer?

My answer is: Yes!

But I'm getting ahead of myself. Let me start at the beginning.

For the past twenty years I have worked with brain-injured children. In 1953 I was fortunate enough to be invited, as a young educator and psychologist, to join a rehabilitation team composed of Dr. Temple Fay—the famed neurosurgeon—and his associates, Glenn Doman and Dr. Robert Doman. Our team became sadly depleted with Fay's death in 1963, but our work continued at The Institutes for the Achievement of Human Potential in Philadelphia.

Glenn Doman was the director of the Institutes; Robert was the medical director and I was the associate director. Working as a part of this team was alternately exasperating and exciting, but always full of surprises.

Glenn, a driving force, was full of enthusiasm, insight, and empathy for our brain-injured children. Trained originally as a physical therapist, he was always searching for reasons why brain-injured children's bodies didn't do what they were supposed to do. Over the years, this search led away from immobile and twisted arms and legs back toward the original hurt to the child: the brain.

Bob was a physician who had specialized in physical medicine and rehabilitation. He loved children and they obviously loved him. His soft voice and gentle manner were always reassuring to the children who were drawn to him.

My role was that of relating our children to the normal worlds of education and learning. It was my responsibility to see that our children learned and that they would succeed at school.

We spent innumerable hours hypothesizing about our brain-injured children, especially our failures. Together we often took imaginary journeys through a child's body, routing our trip through his nervous system.

Going back into a child's body, from his arms and legs, through his peripheral nervous system, up through the spine, into the base of the brain, through the ancient and instinctive brain—up into the modern human brain—was an exciting journey. Even more exciting was the imaginary reverse journey from the brain out to the fingers and toes through that complex highway system called the human nervous system.

It was an ancient system, born hundreds of millions of years ago, and evolving ever so slowly into today's human nervous system. It retained many of its ancient and now seemingly unneeded portions; it had many unused spare parts and, above all, it had preserved many more of its mysteries from probing scientists than any other part of the body.

We had taken other trips too. Glenn, Bob, and I had spent years studying normal children and children with brain injury and learning problems in advanced civilizations in North America and around the world, including primitive tribes in Africa and South and Central America, to see how their nervous systems worked. We had studied children on six continents, searching for clues as to how the brain developed.

As a result of our years of research, we concluded that each child had to go through certain natural stages of development. If a child skipped a developmental stage, he did not achieve his full potential. With such a child, we would take him back to the stage he had missed or short-changed. For example, in mobility a child must crawl on his stomach, then creep on his hands and knees before he walks. If he did not, we took him back to the missed, or incomplete, stage and gave him more practice.

We theorized that the brain develops through use and stimulation. We devised a treatment rationale aimed at stimulating the development and organization of the nervous system. The treatment system became widely known as the Doman-Delacato system of treatment.

We ran into problems with others working in the field. At that time brain injury was approached in an all-or-none fashion. You were brain-injured or not, based on the then accepted neurological tests.

Treatment for brain injury was also an all-or-none affair. If you had it, there was no hope. If you didn't, you were normal.

We proposed that brain injury existed in degrees and that there could be varying degrees of results in working with such children. It was not an all-or-none problem, and treatment need not be based on a hopeless-normal choice. Under the former approach, all those declared hopeless were destined to failure, for no one, except the rare fanatic parent, would attempt to change the child's condition.

We also proposed that new tools were needed to measure brain injury in a more refined way, because it existed on a continuum from severe to mild. We proposed, in addition to using the standard neurological examination to diagnose brain injury, that children's development and function in life should also be evaluated. Glenn, Bob, and I spent years devising a developmental profile as an additional tool to be used in assessing brain injury. This profile took into account what a child could and could not do and related him to what was expected of him at his age level.

Using a developmental and functional approach, we could easily see if brain injury were an all-or-none, or hopeless or normal phenomenon. When a child changed we could measure that change on the profile. We could even do things that would speed up the change. This was called treatment.

Our research led us to the obvious conclusion that there were many forms of brain injury, varying from *severe*—which was easily detected, through viewing a child's body and severe lack of function;—to *moderate,* which could be detected by the well-known neurological examinations using the modern technology of medicine, such as measuring brain waves, checking reflexes and seeking pathological signs—to *mild.* The mild injuries were the most difficult to detect. There were no known measuring tools for their detection. The most common factor in mild brain injury proved to be perceptual problems: *There was apparent difficulty in the way a child took in the world through his eyes, ears, and/or skin.*

Luckily, there were others also working in the field at this time. The condition was rapidly becoming known as "minimal brain injury." A new term came into common use:

soft signs. These were the indications of mild brain injury that could not be demonstrated by the then developed neurological tests. There developed a common agreement about "soft signs" and minimal brain injury.

The team of Knoblock and Pasamanick wrote extensively on brain injury, and a great impetus was given to the subject through the writings of Dr. Sam Clements of the University of Arkansas.[1]

Finally, the U. S. Department of Health, Education, and Welfare published a definitive pamphlet entitled *Minimal Brain Dysfunction in Children* in 1966. Now, minimal brain injury was an accepted concept. Its final result was always apparent in how the child took in the world through his eyes, ears, and skin and also related to how active the child was. The term hyperactivity was now becoming more commonplace when describing children's behavior, especially that of brain-injured children.

These were exciting days of exploring new frontiers in human development that for centuries had been neglected. Perhaps through our work and the work of others, brain-injured children, whether their condition was severe, moderate, or mild, might have a better opportunity to develop into higher levels than had been possible in the past. We were full of enthusiasm and hope.

In 1959 I wrote my first book, which introduced the concept of "neurological organization." The concept stated that the organization and development of the human nervous system was the most important factor in learning. The reaction was immediate—loud—and critical. My subsequent books were also quite controversial. The ideas in them were also attacked.

[1] Clements, S.; Lehtinen, L.; and Lukens, J., *Children with Minimal Brain Injury* (Chicago: National Society for Crippled Children and Adults, 1963).

After an especially vituperative attack on the theory of neurological organization, it was decided that we would have to "cut back" and "regroup" in the interests of self-preservation. It sounded ominous, and it was! After a study of our roles, it was decided that it was no longer possible for me to deal with the problems of reading and learning alone. I was to be involved with a larger problem, that of abnormal behavior.

This meant that I had to turn over to my assistants the handling of the treatment and learning problems, and I was faced with the necessity of tackling the now recognized greater problem, that of abnormal behavior.

I was devastated! After twenty years, all of my work, all of my successes, all of my theories and practices, which were just becoming accepted by schools and clinics throughout the country, were to be turned over to assistants, and I was to walk into a new and unknown world. What did I know about abnormal behavior?

More brain-injured children were coming to us who could walk. But many couldn't talk, couldn't understand spoken words, couldn't be left alone for ten seconds because they were wildly hyperactive. In short, they couldn't do anything that could be considered a human act. They had moderate brain injury but they were severe behavior problems.

These were now *my children*. These youngsters were a far cry from the children with reading and learning problems to whom I was accustomed, and who were now joyfully treated by my assistants. After more than twenty successful years, I had to again become a pioneer. I didn't even know where to start!

The staff, trying to reassure me, smilingly said, "Carl, all of your research on human development and your re-

8   THE ULTIMATE STRANGER

search with primitives and learning, give you a head start
in solving the problem of behavior."

"We envy you. You're going into a whole new field," they
reassured me.

"Carl, we desperately need some solid understanding in
the field of behavior. Think how many kids there are who
might possibly be helped who now exist in a living death."
They tweaked my conscience.

"You've always been a pioneer, Carl. Here's the opportunity to start all over again in your special field of psychology—and there is no competition."

I heard all of the clichés, but none of this eased my mind
or helped.

The powers-that-be, no doubt sensing my frustration
and my panic, provided me with a large, thick-rugged office overlooking a lush green valley and equipped it with
what is probably one of the world's largest desks. In addition, they provided me with an exhaustive library on behavior.

But none of this helped. I was taken from my own hard-
won field, where I was successful, recognized, and well-
known, and now I had to start all over again!

Sensing that I might get up and run at the first opportunity, the powers-that-be threw in a "hooker." He was
Dr. Raymond A. Dart, the world-renowned anthropologist,
a man whom I had long admired and respected. Dart, the
great genius, was to sit at my side daily! I suppose the back-
room thinking was, "He won't run with Dart sitting at his
side."

Dart is an exceptional man. Born and educated as a
physician in Australia, he went to England for further
study in anatomy, and from there to become professor of
anatomy and then the dean at the medical school of the

University of the Witwatersrand in Johannesburg, South Africa.

In late 1924, the year after I was born, a woman, one of Dart's anatomy students, had been instrumental in his receiving a skull found imbedded in a limestone cave.

With his wife's knitting needles, Dart carefully removed the limestone from the petrified image of the brain in this partial skull. In 1925 he wrote an article stating that this was the skull and brain of man's earliest ancestor, whom he called *Australopithecus africanus*. The reaction of the world's scientific community was immediate—and explosive. Everybody knew that man was born in Asia about a hundred thousand years ago! And now the young upstart anatomist was saying that man was born in Africa more than one million years ago! Dart was a fool! To put this totally negative reaction into perspective, you must realize that Dart's original article announcing *Australopithecus africanus* appeared in *Nature* magazine in February 1925 and that the Scopes trial started in the summer of the same year.

Dart spent the next thirty years continuing his anthropological investigations. The veteran South African paleontologist, Robert Broom, found adult and juvenile Australopithecines. Dart and Broom learned all they could about the accompanying animals, and Dart became a menace to then current archaeological theory by showing that *Australopithecus* had pre-Stone Age tools made of bones and teeth. He continued to write, ignoring the constant maelstrom of criticism surrounding him.

Now, forty years later, as a result of the late Louis Leakey's confirming finds at Olduvai; because of potassium argon dating for verification; and finally, with the exposure of fradulent Piltdown Man, Dart was a hero in scientific circles.

The best-selling book *African Genesis,* by Robert Ardrey, had recently brought Dart his much-deserved and long overdue popular acclaim.

This courageous and knowledgeable scientist was to sit by my side daily and, I must admit, the powers-that-be were correct. How could one run away with such a symbol of patience and courage sitting at one's side?

In addition to these qualities and his ultimate victory over his detractors, Dart had other strengths. As the dean of the medical school for twenty years, he had much experience in dealing with youthful enthusiasm and youthful feelings of inadequacy. He also knew more comparative neurology than anyone I had known since death had taken Temple Fay from our midst.

I first met Dart in his adopted country of South Africa in 1966. He had recently retired as dean of the medical school and was now ready for new worlds of challenge. Although in his late seventies when we first met, he was as enthusiastic and as curious as any man I had ever met. He walked briskly with his head thrust forward, his blue eyes sparkling. His Australian accent and his wry wit seemed to keep me both amazed and amused.

Although separated by more than thirty years of age, we reacted to each other remarkably well. Our daily conversations ranged over multitudes of subjects, often punctuated by loud laughter, or long silences—depending on our subject of discussion.

Grudgingly, I had to admit that it was a brilliant stroke to place Dart at my side—he taught me so much.

The powers-that-be were not to be denied. They brought another powerful force into play. He was Dr. Raymundo Veras, medical director of all of our South American institutes. On one of his periodic trips from Brazil, Veras embraced me and, in his newly acquired English, said, "Carl, my brother, I must talk and you must be a good boy and listen."

To hear this from a former student whom I had called a "swarthy giant" and a "mad Buddha" was ominous indeed. Veras and I had fallen in love with each other long before we could communicate with words. I had described him as follows:

> "He was a giant. His thick neck, his heavy arms, his swarthy skin, his black eyes alternating between being too dry with intensity and too moist with sadness, and his total inability to speak one word of English, made our first physician student quite a challenge."[2]

Veras had come to us in 1959 because his only son had broken his neck diving into the Bay of Rio de Janeiro. The boy was completely paralyzed from the neck down. Veras spent a year studying our techniques and watching us treat his teen-age son. Even though he was a renowned surgeon in his native Brazil, Veras worked hard at all kinds of assignments, many of them menial.

As his son improved, Veras made a dramatic decision. He would give up his lucrative practice to introduce our concepts of treating brain injury to Brazil. During the ensuing years, his successes had made him the best-known rehabilitationist in South America.

He remained a very close friend and coworker over the years, constantly helping us to solve problems of brain injury and always joining us in our research with primitive peoples. On three occasions his powerful arms had lifted me out of steaming piranha- and crocodile-infested rivers

2 Delacato, C. H., *A New Start for the Child with Reading Problems: A Manual for Parents* (New York: McKay, 1970), p. 36.

in the central jungle of Brazil so that my testing equipment would not be ruined. He always laughed as he rescued me. His yearly visits to us were always fun-filled and happy. But today he was serious.

And now this too-serious man, whose son had gone on to become a physician and also join us in our work, was to apply his unique type of pressure. I had to listen.

"Carl, you must accept this challenge. In the world today the behavior of man becomes more important and must be understood if we are to survive. To understand these children, with severe behavior problems, can help us to understand all children of all people, and you must help the children of all people. Then, perhaps, Carl, you will better understand yourself and your fellow man."

I fidgeted uncomfortably in my chair, but he hadn't finished.

"You must also go again to talk to your friends Morris and Ardrey, because they know much about the behavior of man, and you can learn from them more about the behavior of children. Carl, you must not think about this more, you must start work now. You must write to me of your findings."

Even with his problems with English, he was always eloquent, and always convincing.

The "Morris" and "Ardrey" to whom he referred were Desmond Morris, author of *The Naked Ape, The Human Zoo,* and *Intimate Behavior;* and Robert Ardrey, author of *African Genesis, Territorial Imperative,* and *The Social Contract.* These men were the leaders of a new field of thought: ethology. Their books had started a revolution in scientific thinking. They had placed man in his proper evolutionary niche, and, through their understanding of other creatures who preceded man, they gave us new insights into ourselves.

Because these men had influenced scientific thinking so significantly, Bob, Glenn, and I had met and talked with them. As Veras said, they were our friends, and he was correct. There was much I could learn by rereading their books and by talking to Morris and Ardrey.

It was now obvious to me that I had no choice but to accept my new assignment. I had to go back to see what was already known about behavior and to see what wasn't known. I also had to learn about the current theories and treatments of behavior.

Ever since the concept of minimal brain injury had been popularized, educators were looking at behavior in a different way. *Hyperactivity* was no longer considered a mere result of lack of discipline. It was now considered an indication of the function of the nervous system.

Suddenly, behavior was becoming an important area of investigation. There were those who used drugs to change behavior; those who used conditioning; those who used behavior modification, and those who used psychiatry.

There was no generally-accepted theory of behavior, and most people preferred to work on the milder types of behavior problems. To really understand behavior, one had to see the whole spectrum of behavior—from the most severe behavior problem to the least.

If one can change the behavior of the child with the most difficult disorder, the less severe problems might be more easily understood.

I decided to explore the most difficult behavior problem. There was no trouble finding the most difficult or the most complex. *There was unanimous opinion among those who work with children. The most difficult, the most baffling, the most bizarre, least successfully treated of all behavior problems was the autistic child.*

Kanner, the man who first wrote about autism, enumerated five characteristic features of what he first termed "early infantile autism." The characteristics were:

1. The inability to relate to and to interact with people from the beginning of life.
2. The inability to communicate with others through language.
3. The obsession with maintaining sameness and resisting change.
4. The preoccupation with objects in favor of people.
5. The occasional evidence of good potential for intelligence.

These five characteristics have been accepted generally as describing autistic children, since Kanner first proposed them in 1943.

Physicians faced with the problem of diagnosing children were given the following general indicators of autism by the *Medical World News:*[3]

The child who is excessively anxious without reason.
The child who has no awareness of his own identity.
The child who is generally preoccupied with a particular object.
The child who twirls.
The child who rocks.
The child who walks on tiptoes.
The child who remains rigid for sustained periods.
The child who resists change.
The child who doesn't speak properly for his age.
The child who doesn't speak at all.

[3] "Breaking Through to the Autistic Child." *Medical World News* (October 1966), p. 92.

The child who appears to be seriously retarded but who, on occasion, shows flashes of normal or exceptional intelligence.

Others[4] list additional symptoms of autism, such as:

Histories of prolonged rocking and/or head banging.
Obsessive interest in certain toys.
Repetitive play.
Insistance on being left alone.
Failure to cooperate and to make anticipatory movements when being picked up.

There is a general agreement that autism is the most baffling of behavioral disorders. It is generally considered to be a psychotic condition characterized by severe withdrawal from the environment. There is also general agreement that the prognosis for the autistic child is extremely poor.

It was obvious that this was the place to start: the autistic child! I did not know enough about diagnosing such children, so I took the easy way out. I used those children who had been diagnosed as autistic by some other professional before the child came to see us. I would see what autistic children looked like up close and not through textbook descriptions.

Steeled by my new and impressive office, buttressed by my exhaustive behavioral library, and buoyed up by my seventy-eight-year-old strong and battlewise companion, Dart, I was ready for anything.

Well, almost anything. I certainly wasn't ready for what came in the door of my office.

[4] Blackwell, R. and Joynt, R., *Learning Disabilities Handbook for Teachers* (Springfield, Ill.: Charles C Thomas, 1972), pp. 42 and 43.

II
REFRIGERATOR MOTHERS?

Six-year-old Bobby walked into my office followed by his sad-eyed parents. His face was ashen gray, and he looked right through me. He walked around my desk constantly waving his right hand a few inches from the lower portion of his face, as though fanning himself. He wasn't destructive, he just walked around with his hand waving in front of his face, staring into space.

His parents sat down; he finally sat between them. Across the desk, I leaned back in my chair and lit a cigarette. He stared at the smoke, his hand still waving in front of his face. Looking at him sitting there, I wondered what was going through his mind, as he alternately stared at the smoke and then right through me. He was oppressively silent. I sat back and waited.

He became more intrigued with my smoke. Hoping I could make *some* contact with him, I started to blow smoke rings. He looked! His hand stopped waving. He stood up, mouth open, staring at the smoke rings.

His parents reported that he had had many diagnoses: mentally retarded; autistic; put him away; and now the most recent, made by our staff: brain injury. Could we help? I said we would try.

Bobby was now about ten feet away from me, not waving his hand in front of his mouth and nose. I wondered if it were a breeze he had been making.

I would try to establish a contact by blowing at him across the room. I took a deep breath, pursed my lips, and blew a long, gentle stream of air at him from across the room.

For a fleeting moment his eyes met mine. There was a trace of a smile on his face as he vomited all over my new rug.

Ann was a beautiful ten-year-old. Her mother walked Ann, who was wearing a football helmet, into my office. She restrained both of Ann's hands behind the child's back. Her mother sat her down, constantly holding Ann's two hands cupped in her own.

Ann had been diagnosed autistic and schizophrenic and mentally retarded, reported her mother. But this child was different. Occasionally she would look at me with a Mona Lisa smile.

Her mother described the symptoms. Ann hit her head with her fists, which accounted for the football helmet. If her mother held both hands, Ann didn't hit as much.

I could see that under the football helmet Ann's forehead was covered with ugly bruises. I asked if I could see the bruises. The mother was delighted. Maybe I wouldn't say Ann was hopeless. Maybe I would *not* suggest an institution. At least, I was interested enough to look at the bruises. I was comforted by the mother's faith.

Gently she took off the football helmet, still holding both of Ann's hands so she wouldn't hit herself. I went closer and looked at the headful of bumps and bruises.

The child smiled warmly at me. I smiled back. Even while she smiled she violently banged her forehead on my desk, with such force that everything in the room seemed to rattle, including me. She had opened a huge gash in her head.

Her remarkably calm mother apologized for the blood that had splattered all over. I assured her that the blood would come out of my suit, the medical records, and, of course, the rug.

Ann smiled again as one of our physicians took her to sew up her scalp.

Jerry was a husky teen-ager. He came into my office like a whirlwind. It wasn't that he moved around very much, he was just noisy. He made a constant hissing sound. His parents held him in his chair. He hissed and occasionally growled.

Former diagnoses were: autism; psychotic; severe mental retardation. These children always seemed to arrive with many different diagnoses.

I noticed that the hissing was becoming more urgent and his growls seemed more threatening. I suggested that the parents allow him to get up and move about the room.

He went to a file cabinet and started to slam the top drawer, in and out. He then picked up a lamp, lifted it six inches, and let it drop on my table, each time with a resounding crash. He picked up my beautiful Swedish ashtray. It was heavy. He lifted it up about eight inches and let it drop with a resounding splatter of glass all over my desk. He ran for the door and, grabbing it in a vicelike grip, began slamming it until every office in the building reverberated with each ear-splitting slam.

Jerry's father and mother tried to stop him. He screamed, pushed them away, and slammed the door.

As a country boy I had learned how to whistle, placing two fingers over my tongue. Maybe a piercing loud whistle might make a contact. I whistled. Jerry looked at me and, as if he had been shot, he crumpled into a hysterical ball of humanity, screaming and writhing as if in great pain. He was hysterical for twenty minutes.

Three months later he walked into my office again. He was a bit quieter. I took out a cigarette. He watched my hands warily. As my hand went to my mouth to place the cigarette between my lips, he blanched. He fell to the floor in wild hysterics. He thought I was going to place my fingers in my mouth again to whistle. In the middle of his hysteria he threw up on my rug.

Andy was a beautiful child. He walked into my office with his parents, sat down, and stared at my phone. Quietly, he got up, came over to my side of the desk and efficiently but quietly began rubbing my phone with a wet facecloth he was carrying.

His mother looked at me panic-stricken and shouted, "Andy, stop that." Before she could get to him I asked her in an authoritarian tone to leave Andy alone. She sat down, quite upset with Andy and me.

Andy next began to shine my new desk with his wet cloth. He seemed very happy. Each time his mother attempted to say something, I would raise my hand in protest. "Please don't talk, I want to observe him," I said sternly.

Periodically Andy would get down on his hands and knees to rest from his polishing task. Then he would go back to work, polishing all the furniture with his damp cloth.

As he started to polish the paneled walls, I wondered why his mother was so tense. Why was she so eager to talk, to interrupt Andy's quiet polishing of everything in my room with his wet cloth?

Andy was ready for another rest, and he went down under my desk. This time I would watch him rest. I walked around the desk and knelt down next to Andy.

He was urinating into the cloth. He had spent the past twenty minutes washing my entire office with his carefully metered-out urine.

Susan was well dressed, with a long-sleeved blouse on this hot day. She was an eight-year-old, and she always wore white cotton gloves. The gloves were not a mark of being dressed up, but rather, a cover for her hands, which she bit constantly, not only when angry and frustrated, but any time. I had never seen her bite her hands. In my office she was ladylike and cooperative. She kept her gloves on. She didn't bite.

I asked her to show me how she bit her hands. She smiled demurely, but refused. I asked to see her scarred hands. She crossed them defiantly and shook her head negatively. Her parents pressed her; she became resistant; they insisted. She put her gloved right hand into her mouth and bit. I could hear her teeth grind on the bone. She bit hard! Her parents ignored it; soon she stopped.

Her parents talked. Was there anything that could be done? Why were there so many diagnoses? What was mental retardation? What was autism?

Her father lit a cigarette. She watched calmly as we talked. Her father wanted to take notes. He put his half-smoked cigarette in the ashtray in front of him and began to write.

She lunged at the cigarette and jammed it down on her right forearm. It burned a hole in her sleeve.

The smell of burning flesh made me feel slightly nauseous. She smiled, sat back, and listened.

These were the autistic children with their extremely alien behavior. If I could find an answer for these unfortunate children, all other behavior problems might fall into some logical pattern.

I watched these children and I watched their mothers. Was there a clue in their mothers?

Autism is a disease with an early onset. The single most important factor in the environment for these children is their mothers.

Quickly I went back to my new library. I read everything I could about the *cause* of the problem. As I read, the cause seemed to reduce itself to the fact that these children were the result of *"refrigerator parents,"* especially a *"refrigerator mother."*

I went back to the original article written on the subject of autism. Dr. Leo Kanner, a psychiatrist on the staff of Johns Hopkins Hospital, was the first person who saw these children as a unique group. His first article on the subject of autism appeared thirty years ago (1943) in *Pathology* and was titled, "Autistic Disturbances of Affective Content."

Dr. Kanner concluded at that time that the problem was caused by psychological factors, primarily the aloofness of the parents and their lack of warmth toward the child.

In describing early infantile autism in following articles, Kanner stated that it was a response to "living in an emotional refrigerator."

Kanner[1] felt that most of the patients were exposed to parental coldness. They were given very little warmth of

[1] Kanner, L., "Problems of Nosology and Psycho Dynamics of Early Infantile Autism." *American Journal of Orthopsychiatry* 19:426 (1949).

reaction. He likened the situation for these children to being kept in refrigerators that did not defrost.

I talked to a number of people who worked with autistic children. They were almost unanimous in their feeling: *"Autism is a form of psychosis, caused by refrigerator mothers."*

By this time I had observed over one hundred children who had autism as at least one of their diagnoses. I could not agree that their parents, especially their mothers, were any less emotionally involved or were any "colder" than those of the other children I treated.

Many of those "in the field" referred me to the writings of Bruno Bettleheim. In his book *The Empty Fortress*,[2] Bettleheim proposes that the interaction of the mother and baby while the baby is at the breast is of great significance in the baby's development of self. He feels that interference with this interaction, because of the mother's lack of responsiveness to her baby, can be responsible for causing autistic disturbances in children. Bettleheim's approach is psychoanalytic. He feels that nursing is the central experience for the child, from which develop later feelings about oneself and others. Bettleheim contends that nursing must represent an interaction between mother and child and that the way in which the mother holds the child and reacts to the child is of great significance—a warm, mutual response creating emotional satisfaction for the child; no response, or a cold response, provoking an impotent rage. The psychoanalytical approach suggests that if this interaction while nursing is not satisfying to the child, the inner rage and inner tension cause the types of disturbances one sees in the autistic child.

Other authors with a psychoanalytic bias went even

[2] Bettleheim, B., *The Empty Fortress* (New York: The Free Press, 1967), pp. 14, 15, 17, 19, and 46.

farther. They localized the problem to the nipple. They mention those autistic children who fight at the breast. They blame this fighting on the fact that the fatty breast cut off the child's air supply while he sucked. He fought, not to avoid sucking, but to get more air. Some blame this, in part, as a causative factor in autism.

Gunther[3] states that babies who have suffered such an air blockage, whether by the baby's upper lip going over the nostrils or by the breast covering the nostrils, cry and box themselves off the breast as a protest against the air blockage.

I watched mothers with their autistic children. I could not believe that these were passive, cold, or noninteractive mothers when I saw them with their children.

This talk of nipples and refrigerator mothers bothered me. These mothers seemed warm, caring, and they exhibited no paucity, or uniqueness, in the breast or nipple area.

Could it be that these frightening behaviors had clouded our vision? Even as to cause? Why should we blame these mothers? Did we have real evidence or just theory?

If these mothers were cold and were off base in nipple use, what about *their normal children?* They seemed to have survived and to have developed normally. Could a mother be cold and nonreacting while nursing one of her children without being the same while nursing her other children? Why were the others in the family normal children?

During my research with primitive tribes in Africa and South America, I had observed hundreds of babies at the breast, but my conclusions about breasts were in disagreement with the psychoanalytic school of thought.

[3] Gunther, M., "Infant Behavior at the Breast," in Foss, B. M. (ed.), *Determinants of Infant Behavior* (London: Metheun, 1961).

While living with the Bushmen in the Kalahari Desert,
I noticed that as a Bushwoman begins her child-bearing
career, her breasts become extremely elongated and pendulous. I have seen many Bushwomen's breasts that extended
well below the navel.

Bush children treat these breasts like long rubber tubes
that supply milk. I have seen Bush children walking
around their mothers, extending the breast under the arm-
pit and back behind the mother, without missing a single
suck in their feeding rhythm. There was no interaction
between mother and child, except an occasional ill-
tempered howl when the mother stood up and walked
away or unceremoniously pulled the breast out of the
child's mouth.

Bush nipples are very large and Bush breasts are very
long, yet I saw no fighting at the breast. Interestingly
enough, I never saw a brain-injured or an autistic Bush
child.

The same is true of Xingu mothers, whom I had studied
on numerous occasions in the central jungles of Brazil.
These mothers do not have the long, pendulous breasts of
the Bushwomen. They do not have a Madonnalike inter-
active breast-feeding position, but instead, are very likely
to gossip or dig roots while their infant goes through an
on-again, off-again struggle to suck at the breast. As the
children grow older, their sucking becomes even more pre-
carious and uninvolved. Neither mother nor child seems
particularly involved; the child persists because of hunger.

I never saw a brain-injured or an autistic child in the
Xingu territory during any of my four stays, or in any of
the tribes I studied.

But none of this helped, for the consensus of the experts
about the cause of autism could be reduced to "refrigerator

mothers," and that coldness was reduced by some to the way in which the child was allowed to have the breast and nipple. I was at a dead end.

Breasts were a blind alley. I could not agree with the "refrigerator" or "breast" theory. These women were scapegoats.

Once again I had arrived at a point where I just could not agree with the "experts." Their evidence was nonexistent. It was a theory, based on very little demonstrable fact.

I sat at my desk and slowly opened my mail. What if the "experts" were right? If they were, why didn't they offer some proof instead of just theory?

I opened a letter from a mother of one of our autistic children. It contained an article entitled "Parents as Scapegoats" from *Human Behavior* magazine.[4]

As I read, I learned why this mother had sent me the article.

"Ancient Jewish ritual called for banishment of an innocent goat into the wilderness after the chief priest of the Day of Atonement had symbolically saddled it with all the sins of the people. A modern scientific parallel finds a preponderance of psychotherapists religiously conferring a clinical absolution upon autistic and psychotic children by making scapegoats of their parents.

"Mental health specialists have been all too quick to embrace the dogma that a child's emotional withdrawal and ego disorganization invariably can be traced to parental behavior."

The article even mentioned the fear and agony visited upon the Salem witches. It likened the treatment of parents to the treatment received by those unfortunate women in Salem.

[4] *Human Behavior* I(3):8 (1972).

As I completed reading the article, Dart entered my room for our daily afternoon session.

"Sir," I asked, "may I read you an article?"

Dart stared out the window into the valley as I read the article to him. "Sir, I agree with him. These mothers are scapegoats. I can't agree with all this talk about nipples, breasts, and refrigerator mothers without more evidence. The article even goes on to mention the fact that the rejection of women has been with us historically back to the Salem witch trials."

Dart turned toward me, his head bent forward, as it always was when he concentrated. "Carl, you need to know much more about women. Men have always been so fully dependent upon women for their growth and strength—in the womb, at the breast, as well as at the daily table—that they unconsciously resent, and at the same time are fascinated by, those symbols of their early frailty and dependence—such as wombs and breasts.

"You, personally, have seen menstruating women banned from their tribes until the menstrual flow ceased, all in the guise of improving the males in hunting. You must learn more about man's rejection of woman in times of stress or lack of understanding.

"As a beginning, read about your Salem witch trials. Then go back and read the sordid history of witch hunting in Europe that preceded, all coming from the Biblical admonition 'Thou shalt not suffer a witch to live'" (Exodus 22:18).

I acquiesced as politely as I could, but I wasn't enthusiastic.

What I found was indeed frightening. Witches have been on man's mind for thousands of years. Witch hunting has been an activity of righteous men since Biblical times, reaching its apex during the Middle Ages and continuing until very recently. A few years before the discovery of America a standard Inquisition handbook for the tracking-down of witches was published. It presumed guilt and, as a result, advocated any mode of torture or trickery to obtain a confession. All of this followed the Bull of Pope Innocent VIII condemning witches in 1484.

"The coming of Calvinism, with its belief in human depravity and Satanic power, added further impetus to the Inquisition. Torturing and burning was the rule. Special witch jails were built. Nine hundred witches were destroyed in a single year in the Wurtzberg area, and a thousand in and around Como. At Toulouse, four hundred people were put to death in a single day."[5]

Whenever there was a stress on the culture, such as famine or plague, witch hunting increased. The phenomenon moved to England, where the peak of witch hunting occurred during the early seventeenth century. The Pilgrims carried their witch-hunting notions to the New World.

Witchcraft was tied to a "fertility-sterility" conflict, and Pope Innocent's Bull made it clear that witches were responsible for increasing sterility. Indeed, a constant charge against witches was that they stole men's penises or, worse still, rendered them unfunctional.

There was much concern with witches and their relationship to animals. They became overly "familiar" with their animals, especially cats. This "familiarity" was often thought to be expressed through their suckling such animals from their breasts. Such suckled animals were usually cats.

The *Lawes against Witches and Conivration*, published

[5] Tindall, G., *A Handbook on Witches* (New York: Atheneum, 1966), p. 21.

in 1645 by "authority," stated that: "their said Familiar hath some big or little Teat upon their body, where he sucketh them."[6]

A cat so suckled became, in essence, a "familiar" or a stand-in for the witch and could carry out the witch's magic in the community. In England the cat was usually black.

As a result of dealing with "familiars," witches were thought to have supernumerary breasts, and one of the most incriminating signs of witchcraft was to have a growth anywhere on the body that had anything resembling a teat on it.

We will never know how many women were burned at the stake because their piles, old warts, fistulas, moles, and scars looked as though they ended in a teat.

These supernumerary breasts were tested by inserting needles in them to see if they were warm-blooded and bled, or were cold-blooded and didn't bleed.

As time went on, and especially in Salem, the diagnosis of a witch became more sophisticated. One needed only to look at the nipple: If it were inverted, it signified that its owner was a witch. Next, instead of sticking the breast with a pin, it was now felt. If warm, it was not the breast of a witch. If cold, it presented rather positive proof that one had uncovered a witch.

From this more sophisticated approach, we Americans gained a new way to describe cold. From that time on things became "cold as a witch's tit."

I now knew why Dart had sent me back to read about witches. Here we were again at nipples, inverted or not, and breasts, warm or cold.

How familiar this sounded! Was it possible that in our more civilized time we used the same criteria for blaming

[6] Murray, M., *The Witch Cult in Western Europe* (London: Oxford University Press, 1921), p. 86.

the mothers of autistic children? Today we don't look at a mother's nipples to see if they are inverted or protrude, but we accuse her of misuse of her nipples with her progeny, thus causing this terrible alienation.

Today we don't feel the mother's breast and call her "cold-titted." Instead, we call her a "refrigerator mother" and blame her for her child's alienation.

Although we are more civilized in our use of words, are we using the same terrible concepts to blame the mothers for creating aliens in our midst?

And now my work had to start in earnest. Were these myths, these superstitions still clouding our thinking, even as to the cause of the child's problem? Perhaps I could introduce some light into this *alien* world. I had to search for a more rational answer. I owed it to those mothers who had come to me for help.

III
THE DIVINE DISEASE

Dr. Leo Kanner first put the term "autism" into the modern medical literature in 1943. Although first pointed out as a syndrome in 1943, the problem has been with us historically, but under different names. Hippocrates and other great Greek physicians grouped in the category of "divine diseases" those severe and unexplainable behavior problems ranging from convulsions to strange and unpredictable behavior. The implication was that there was something *other* than the physical involved in the problem. Since they were not understood, there was also an aura of the "possessed" surrounding such diseases.

Historically, there has always been a differentiation made by cultures when dealing with children with strange problems. Children who were slow or who could not learn to survive in their cultures were treated as "the village idiots." Such children were tolerated with considerable care and affection as long as their behavior did not interfere with the normal life of the village.

Children with more severe behavior problems were not so fortunate. They were too different. Nothing about their behavior was predictable or understandable. In addition, the usual approaches to behavior control, such as reward and punishment, did not work. These children were looked upon as being possessed or controlled by some strange incomprehensible force. They were assumed to be under demonic possession. They couldn't be ignored.

During Biblical times, such children were often taken to the healers to see if their behavior could be changed through some divine interference. The healers attempted to "cast out the evil spirits" or to "cleanse them." If the demon's control could be removed, the child could once again resume control of his own behavior and, naturally, he would act like other children.

During Greek and Roman times, such children were occasionally sewed into the wet skin of a goat (*capra,* from which we derive the word "capricious") in an attempt to calm down their strange behavior. The goat skin, as it dried and shrank, served as a forerunner of the straitjacket. During the entire pre-Christian era, when the healers failed and when fear, force, and inflicted pain failed, *abandonment* became the final treatment method.

During the early Christian period and during the Middle Ages, these children suffered greatly. This was the height of the "possessed" approach. Such children were approached religiously. If religion could not cure the problem, the next step was excoriating the problem through fear and punishment, such as chaining, beating, and mutilating. These were the days of the snake pit approach to problems of behavior. Shock and fear of pain would cure all. There were even some strange cases of worship of these unfortunate children. Since they acted as though possessed, they were either possessed by the devil or by God. If by the devil, they were terribly mistreated; if by God, they were venerated. Needless to say, most were deemed possessed by the devil. Because of the new values and attitudes introduced to the culture by Christianity, abandonment was only acceptable when all else failed. Few children survived the punishment treatment to reach the abandonment stage.

With the advent of the Industrial Revolution, a new value was put on children: money. They could now work in factories or mines and earn money. Besides, the discipline and work were considered good for their character and for their souls. Even mild behavior deviations became intolerable. The child with obvious behavior deviations was dealt with physically and severely: "for his own good and for the salvation of his soul."

Bedlam, the first mental institution, was a significant breakthrough. At least the adults with strange behavior were no longer considered possessed or willfully malingering. Now they were considered sick. They could live in Bedlam and, incidentally, be protected from a culture bent on punishment. Shocking as our image of Bedlam may be, it was the nearest to a humane form of abandonment that men devised at that time.

During the past century Freud taught us that the psyche had been overlooked in the search to cure man's ills, especially his behavioral ills. Freud's influence upon the world's thinking will never be totally known, for he helped men turn their eyes inward, seeking the hidden causes of the illness within themselves. Indeed, if a person seemed "possessed," it was by his own sick inner being. This sickness was caused, according to Freud, by the lack of fulfillment of certain drives for pleasure and satisfaction. This frustration and lack of fulfillment led to an inner anger. It was this inner rage that created the sickness.

He proposed that in treatment we must expose this inner rage, look at it rationally, look at its cause, and understand it, and the sickness would be controlled. Freud sensitized man to his own psyche or inner being, so that it was recognized that man is both a physical and a psychic being, and that these two systems very significantly influence each other.

Freud's great insights helped man to make a giant step forward in his knowledge of himself. His insights are at times misused, however, because whenever we cannot find an adequate physical answer to a problem, we too often give it a psychic label, by default.

Since Freud there have been many breakthroughs in the knowledge about the human body, and with many of the physiological breakthroughs we have decreased what were formerly considered psychic ills. Convulsive seizures were, at one time, considered the result of being possessed, next they were considered a form of hysteria, and today they are considered the result of faulty electrical discharges within the brain, usually the result of brain injury. The diabetic coma was at one time considered a form of being possessed; later it was considered a form of hysteria, because people seemed to go into one and come out for no apparent reason; and today they are controlled through the understanding that they are the result of a faulty insulin-sugar balance in the body.

Historically, as man learned more about the chemical, electrical, and physical functioning of his body, his understanding helped him to appreciate physical relationships to behavior that he could not heretofore understand.

Since at the outset we had no clearly defined physical cause for autistic behavior, it was natural that the Freudian view of inner rage was the first explanation given for autistic behavior. Since this view has not resulted in significant breakthroughs in treatment, other explanations had to be sought.

After his 1943 article, Kanner continued to write about autism. Many others joined the search for more answers, and autism became a commonly used word. Scientists in other nations joined the search. There was general agreement during the 1940s that Kanner had defined a new disease and that it was a form of psychosis.

During these early years little was said about treatment. What was offered as treatment was offered quite tentatively and pessimistically. Treatment was psychiatric. It usually took the form of loving handling of the child, play therapy for the child, and/or counseling for the parents. Hundreds of articles were written about autism. Many diagnostic views were expressed. The large number of articles was an indication of the great interest in the subject and in the groping for understanding that went on.[1]

During the early 1950s and 1960s a few writers began to raise questions about the difficulty and the validity of diagnosis. There were a great number of articles written in attempts to differentiate autism from childhood schizophrenia and/or mental retardation. Because there were so many similarities between the autistic and what was termed "early childhood schizophrenia," the diagnoses often overlapped. There was also overlap with children considered mentally retarded. Rimland pointed out that the diagnostic process for autistic children was hopelessly muddied.[2]

A new note began to creep into the articles written about autism. *Was it really a disease with a psychological cause, or did it have some physical or organic basis?*

A few of the leaders in the field thought that there was some physical cause. Bender felt that autism was of organic origin. She felt that it was caused by a "diffuse en-

[1] For an overview of the kinds of articles written, see Bibliography.
[2] Rimland, B., *Infantile Autism* (New York: Appleton-Century-Crofts, 1964).

cephalopathy of prenatal origin,"[3] which means a wide-spread lack of brain development before birth. Rimland beautifully illustrated how the symptoms of autism could result from difficulty in giving meaning to incoming sensory stimulation. He felt that there was a basic inability to relate incoming stimulations to related stored information. Rimland attributed the problem to damage to the reticular formation of the brain stem in genetically predisposed infants.[4]

Schopler also related autism to the receptor system.[5] He felt that the autistic child had not moved from using near receptors (taste, smell, feel) to the distance receptors of seeing and hearing. Because these children do not make this transition, they remain at the near receptor level of function. Schopler thought that this inability was the result of sensory deprivation of the child. He felt that the sensory deprivation was the result of an *inborn deficiency* of the nervous system of the child, coupled with a mother who tended to understimulate her child. He combined the causes so that they were sensory and genetic.

I could not accept the genetic implication of Rimland's or Schopler's positions. The science of genetics has, since the time it was originated by Mendel, evolved into a science of prediction. It is a science of mathematics and formulas —all aimed at the prediction of genetic traits. True, human beings are much too complex to be predicted genetically in all ways, but genetic trends and patterns can be computed even for human beings. This can be done from generation to generation and within a family.

[3] Bender, L., "The Brain and Child Behavior." *Archives of General Psychiatry* 4:531 (1961).
[4] Rimland, op. cit.
[5] Schopler, E., "Early Infantile Autism and Receptor Processes." *Archives of General Psychiatry* 13:327–37 (1965).

If there were a genetic causative factor in autism, its pattern should be discernible from one generation to the next. Its appearance should follow some formula from generation to generation, and it does not. There is no concrete evidence indicating a generation-to-generation incidence of autism.

Since there is no generational evidence, one might question whether autism exists as a cluster within single families. One could question whether there was a pattern of other children in the same family who were autistic. There is no concrete evidence relative to the clustering of the incidence of autism within single families or from generation to generation.

There was no unanimity of opinion as to causes of autism. Although the great majority felt that the problem was psychogenic, there were a few others in the field who felt that it was physical and inherited.

One psychiatrist-father of an autistic child differentiated the approaches even more clearly in his article, "The Two Camps in Child Psychiatry: A Report from a Psychiatrist-Father of an Autistic and Retarded Child."[6] He felt as a result of his personal and parental experiences that there were two diagnostic camps:

1. The psychiatric camp, which believed that the problem was caused by psychological factors. This camp dismissed any organic or physical causes.

2. The physiologic-organic group. This group felt that the cause was physical in some way and that the behavior was a result.

As a result of the differences of opinion as to the cause of the problem, different treatment approaches were devised. None of them had proved to be highly successful.

[6] Kysar, J., *American Journal of Psychiatry* I(125):141–46 (1968).

Kanner stated in 1954 that autism *had not been influ-enced* by any form of therapy.[7] In 1956 he wrote that *psychotherapy* seemed, in general, to be of little avail, with few apparent exceptions.[8]

In 1964 Rimland wrote that no form of psychiatric treatment has been known to alter the course of autism.[9]

Many treatment approaches were tried. Some researchers tried negative and/or positive conditioning approaches. Electric shock was used for behavior that was undesirable, and rewards, such as candy, for behavior that was desirable. The National Institutes of Health[10] developed a helmet that gave an electric shock to head-bangers each time they banged their heads.

Other researchers felt that autistic children are in a constant state of high arousal. This high cortical arousal limits sensory inputs to a single set. Some results showed relatively stable EEG (brain waves). When someone entered a room, the EEG reverted to a highly aroused state. These children were treated with drugs—both depressant and excitatory drugs. The results of these experiments were not encouraging. Still others tried educational approaches through special schooling and special training. Still others attempted to modify autistic behavior through dietary and vitamin regimens.

No single approach has provided significant results with these children.

Controlled studies are always called for in validating treatment procedures. In this field *there are no controlled*

---

[7] Kanner, L., "General Concept of Schizophrenia at Different Ages," in *Neurology and Psychiatry in Childhood* (Baltimore: Williams and Wilkins, 1954), pp. 451–53.

[8] Eisenberg, L. and Kanner, L., "Early Infantile Autism, 1943–1955." *American Journal of Orthopsychiatry* 26:556–66 (1956).

[9] Rimland, op. cit.

[10] "Electrified Helmet Strikes Back at Autism." *Medical World News* (January 21, 1971), pp. 27–34.

studies. A few attempts at comparing children fall far short of control in the meager studies done. In short, there is no validated treatment, and those treatments most in vogue had become so simply because they are *some* attempt at helping these children. Whether they do, or not, is a moot question.

The very fact that the treatment approaches are so divergent from each other is an indication that the search for answers is still in a very preliminary stage.

I went to residence institutions for children to see what I could learn. I am always uncomfortable in such institutions, first, because of the hopelessness; second, because I always have difficulty accepting the label of "mental retardation." Too many children thus labeled have symptoms of brain injury. As a result, these unfortunate children are misunderstood and are treated as though they have no potential. If they had been diagnosed as brain-injured, an effort would have been made to help them. Because they have been labeled mentally retarded, they have become our forgotten people. There was almost universally no treatment. Where there was treatment, it didn't work. And too few seemed to care. I was depressed!

Now I was even more disturbed. As I watched the children, who were in reality a mixture of mentally retarded and brain-injured, suddenly I began to see all kinds of repetitive behavior. Why did these children have autisms? Were they *also autistic?*

Would nature give one child *three* catastrophic diseases —all at one time?

Was it possible that these children were all *one type of child* to whom we had given different names?

An even more disturbing fact arose. As I sat in the large waiting room of The Institutes for the Achievement of Hu-

man Potential—which was always crowded with children—
I became increasingly perplexed. These children had mixed
diagnoses upon arrival: mentally retarded, brain injured,
and autistic. They began to appear to me to be more and
more like each other.

Now I could understand why there was such a problem
about diagnosis. There was too much overlap among these
groups. If they were all one group with different labels, I
might fall into the same diagnostic trap. I decided not to
try to diagnose which was which. For my studies, *I would
only accept a child as being "autistic" if some outside authority had previously diagnosed him as autistic* before his
visit to me. *I would not trust my own diagnosis because
the three groups looked too much alike.*

My confusion increased. Perhaps I could find how autistic children were considered *different* by other professionals who wrote about them. I would try to find the
differences referred to and then I would see if those differences existed in brain-injured or mentally retarded
children. This might help me to separate them from each
other.

Most writers about autism mentioned one common
"difference": the need on the part of the autistic children
to preserve *sameness* in their environment. Changes disturb them.

Some writers referred to the writings of Piaget to explain
this need for sameness in their environment. Piaget feels
that children go through seven stages of sensory-motor development. During the fourth stage a child learns to establish the permanence of an object in space. This is where
the autistic child fails, assumes Piaget. To the autistic child,
the object exists only when the child sees it in its usual
place. Here is where the autistic child is lacking in adapta-
bility. The object has no permanence for him unless it is

always in the same place or its existence is re-enforced by touching.

Piaget conducted interesting experiments with children at this stage of development. As such a child was reaching for an object at which he was looking, Piaget interposed his hand between the child's eyes and the object. The child no longer reached for the object. For the child, the object was no longer there.

Piaget theorized that since any logical mental functioning depends on the concept of permanence of objects, the frightened and anxious autistic child, who doesn't achieve the concept of permanence of objects, becomes even more anxious and frightened. In an effort to defend his already highly threatened ego, the autistic child insists on sameness in his environment.[11]

While working with brain-injured children and adults who *had been normal* and had *become* brain-injured through accidents, I had noticed the same need for sameness. Indeed, Glenn Doman and I had written an article describing their need for spatial sameness and even for temporal sameness back in 1956![12] Any changes in furniture or in time schedule were very upsetting to these patients. Our article described how these children and adults developed "spatial and temporal rigidities" because of their brain injury. This rigidity (need for sameness) appeared right after the brain injury, and as the patient progressed, the need for sameness decreased.

But these patients had once been normal and were now

---

[11] Piaget, J., *The Construction of Reality in a Child* (New York: Basic Books, 1954).

[12] Delacato, C. and Doman, G., "Hemiplegia and Concomitant Psychological Phenomenon," *The American Journal of Occupational Therapy*, Vol. X, No. 4, July–August, Part I, 1956.

brain-injured. No one had even considered labeling them autistic—they were brain-injured. This "difference" was not a *real* difference, because we saw it in brain injury of all types. It was, in reality, a sign of brain injury.

Another group informed me that a lack of laterality was a "unique" ingredient of autism. This is the lack of using the right hand, right eye, right ear, and right foot consistently for skills; or the left hand, left eye, left ear, and left foot consistently and exclusively.

I had long known that lack of laterality was the indication of mild brain injury or the lack of organization of the nervous system, resulting in learning and reading problems, and had written four books outlining my theories and findings on the subject of lack of laterality. For twenty years this phenomenon was almost universally evident in my learning "problems." It also involved the brain.

Another "unique" aspect of autism brought to my attention was "hyperactivity." I knew that this could not be unique to this group, for hyperactivity is now discussed constantly by educators when referring to their learning problems. Indeed, it is today one of the most universally accepted "soft signs" of brain injury.

Trying to find the "unique" ingredient of autism was very difficult. Some experts told me that one almost universal sign of autism was "they walk on their toes." This was surprising, because for twenty years we had been working with brain-injured children who walked on *their* toes. Indeed, spasticity in a child *always* resulted in his walking on his toes.

We were not the only group who saw such children. Others who had a more traditional approach to brain-injured children had devised heel cord stretching and bracing to cure toe walking. Indeed, annually, many surgical operations are performed by these groups to lengthen the child's Achilles tendon, so he won't walk on his toes. It was obvious that toe walking was not unique to autistic children; it was a universally accepted sign of brain injury.

The other "difference" most commonly referred to was the repetitive nongoal-directed behaviors that were called "autisms." I was struck by the fact that, although many writers on the subject of the autistic child mentioned the repetitive rhythmic behaviors that they labeled "stereotyped behaviors" or "ritualistic behaviors" or "autisms," very little was said in description or in explanation of these behaviors. Most important, nothing was said or done about treatment.

Much was said about the withdrawal tendency and the lack of speech of these children, but relatively nothing was said about the repetitive behavior. This is even more striking when one first sees a group of autistic children, because such behavior is the one thing that stands out with them. It is this repetitive behavior that makes them unique children. If they did not have these behavior aberrations, they would be like other children who don't talk.

I was intrigued by these "autisms." Furthermore, I was intrigued by the fact that most workers in the field chose to ignore them. I was also intrigued by the fact that it was these behaviors, above all, that the *parents* felt were *the most extreme aspect* of the autistic child's problem. Universally, the parents told me that the repetitive behaviors were what made their child "stand out." The parents all felt that if the "autisms" could be removed, their children might stand a chance. To the parents the repetitive behavior was what was unique.

Furthermore, they felt that when the child was carrying out this repetitive behavior *he was the most withdrawn* in a world of his own making. If only that behavior would stop! Maybe then the child would be closer and more involved with the world around him. Maybe then he could survive.

These repetitive behaviors seemed to be the closest to a "unique" symptom of autism. Perhaps if I learned more about these autisms, I might make a beginning in understanding these children.

IV
BREAKTHROUGH?

These repetitive behaviors are called "autisms." They are considered the stigmata of the autistic child—his trademark, so to speak. As I became more accustomed to observing these autisms, I noticed that whatever form they took, from hand biting to face slapping to twirling, they all contained a repetitive rhythm and that most of them fell within a small range of speeds. That is, most autisms are carried out by most children at the same rate of speed, no matter what form the autism took.

I also noticed that, when the children were carrying out these repetitive acts, they were in a world of their own. They seemed *more distant* and *more detached* from the real world whenever they bit, twirled, slapped, or banged repeatedly. Strangely enough, they also seemed more content during these times.

Perhaps there was a message in the *rhythm*. I decided to look for these rhythmic behaviors in animals. I observed animals individually and in herds in their natural habitats in Africa and South America. There were no repetitive behaviors. I next observed the same types of animals in cages in zoos. Here I did see the repetitive behavior. The same animals who had no repetitive behavior in their natural habitats developed rather severe repetitive behavior mannerisms when in a cage. Some of these mannerisms become so severe that they are self-mutilative.

Desmond Morris refers to these repetitive behaviors as rhythmic stereotypes.[1] He feels that when we suppress the exploratory urge, by placing an animal in a cage, these stereotypes of behavior, which he calls "Anti-exploratory devices," are useful. He feels that they are basically the result of exterior boredom or stress. Could it be boredom or stress that was causing the repetitive behavior in my autistic children? I didn't know.

I observed a number of small infants. In some I noticed a tendency to repetitive behavior. A number of them would rhythmically wave a hand in front of their eyes as they stared into a light or at a window. But they soon outgrew this form of what appeared to be visual play. It seemed as though they needed to go through a stage of this sort of behavior in which they gained practice in seeing the outline of their hand against the light. When they had a short experience with this, they moved on to the next stage of visual development.

I also noticed that infants did the same thing with their voices. They made repetitive sounds with their voices, almost playing with their voices, but they soon outgrew these repetitive sounds and moved on to producing other sounds.

Since so many infants carried out these repetitive acts, one could conclude that they are needed in some way for at least a short period of time. When they have served their purpose, the infant outgrows them and moves on to another kind of activity.

[1] Morris, D., *The Naked Ape* (New York: McGraw-Hill, 1967), pp. 144, 145.

But what was its purpose?

I had once seen a child who had DeLang Syndrome, a condition where the balance mechanism of the brain does not develop completely. Such children have a poorly developed ability to sense changes in balance and have a poor sense of balance, in general, as a result. I noticed that this child would spin incessantly, almost as though he were trying to make himself dizzy, despite his inability to become dizzy or, perhaps, because he was in a constant state of dizziness.

I must be overlooking something. Why would something exist in nature with no previous existence in our millions of years of evolution? Why would it exist only in man? And, most puzzling of all, why did these meaningless repetitive behaviors *not* exist in the primitive groups I studied, but do exist in civilized man?

Could nature have created a *meaningless* dead-end type of behavior that existed only in modern, civilized man?

I would try some of these activities on myself. If I spin around trying to copy an autistic child's spinning, I become dizzy. If I bite my hand in imitation, my hand hurts and I stop biting.

If I flashed lights in the eyes of brain-injured children at a certain rate of speed, they became uncomfortable and, if I persisted, they went into a convulsive seizure. The rhythm had some effect—but it conveyed no meaning. I was at a dead end.

I visited a number of children's mental institutions that contained great numbers of children who were classified as "mentally retarded" by those who had placed them there. These visits always depressed me, for each time I saw children whom I considered brain-injured and *not* mentally retarded. These children were victims of an incorrect diagnosis. I believed they could learn, if given the opportunity.

The most universal, and the most dramatic, behavioral characteristic that I saw in these institutionalized children was their repetitive behavior. Why these children? They couldn't all be psychotic—then why the repetitive behavior?

Rhythmic shaking was a part of the many convulsions that I had seen. Convulsions are a symptom of brain injury. They could be seen via the electroencephalograph, which measures the electrical activity of the brain. When the brain waves become extremely disorganized, a convulsive seizure occurs. But the rhythmic features of a convulsive seizure were of no help. Those children were not even conscious while they carried out their strange repetitive behavior.

I was at another dead end!

The Araguaya River, which flows north toward the Amazon, teams with exotic water life. The evening air was oppressive, the jungle life was becoming quieter; the only exceptions were the occasional raucous shrieks of a macaw and the whirring of pairs of parrots as they took off, in loving husband-and-wife harmony, for the heart of the forest.

Our work was completed, we had eaten a marvelous meal of piranha and beans. I always loved walking along the river, especially in dry season when the river lost its blood-red color and became more tranquil. I took off my boots, dipped my feet into the tepid stream, and started to work on my notes.

I glanced down at my feet and a small, eellike creature was chasing a tiny, silvery fish around my feet. Suddenly, in a burst of survival anxiety, the small fish jumped over my feet out of the water, onto the bank right next to my boots. The eellike creature abandoned the hunt and swam off.

The tiny silvery fish lay there next to my boots breathing heavily, almost in a state of shock. As I watched, I saw the beginning of a twitching of its tail, which gradually encompassed its whole body. The fish was rhythmically moving its whole body—just as the autistic children—with no apparent goal or usefulness involved in the movement.

This continued for almost a full minute. Then my silvery friend went into a wild convulsive flapping of its entire body. There was such force in its convulsive movements that I could hear its tiny body hit the earth. It was obviously hurting itself badly. It would soon die.

It repeated the convulsive flapping and its small body hit the earth so hard that the body bounced and, with a final flap, the tiny fish fell back into the water and swam away. If it had stayed out of the water, it would have died from oxygen starvation. The rhythmic convulsive flapping, although it had appeared nongoal-directed, had saved the creature's life.

Fay had once written an article entitled, "The Other Side of a Fit," in which he concluded that convulsive seizures were originated as a necessity for all animals that lived in water but that, occasionally, got out into the air. The only way for that fish to survive was to get back into the water. The rhythmic flapping and violence of the seizure were nature's mechanism of getting the fish from the land back where it could breathe again, in the water!

Again, Fay's genius had helped. Here was a supposedly meaningless act, which had real meaning. It had saved the silvery fish's life!

Fay had also concluded that the rhythmic convulsive seizure that happens in brain injury is a life-saving activity. It is nature's way of restoring a proper electrochemical balance in the brain and to preserve life. What had been looked upon as the "divine disease" in early times and what was a frightening, seemingly meaningless catastrophic reaction of the organism, appeared to Fay as a life-saving device that we inherited from our fish ancestry. *I had to keep looking for the hidden message.*

Nancy was an habitual hand biter. You could hear her teeth hitting the bones of her hand as she bit. Her right hand was constantly red because of her deep biting.

Today, Nancy didn't bite her hand. Her brother had slammed the car door on her hand and it was black and blue and swollen from the accident. Why hadn't she bitten her hand since the accident? It had been her greatest problem, and now it was gone. Why?

I decided to look at different types of children to see if there were a rhythm factor through which they communicated. One of the groups I visited was in a school for blind children. I arrived at assembly time and, since I was there, I was asked if I would speak to the students.

As I stood looking out over the student body, a strange, uncomfortable feeling came over me, almost as if most of the student body were mocking me. Many of the children were rocking in their chairs, waving their hands in front of their faces, tapping their eyes! I knew all these behaviors were "autisms," but they couldn't be! *These children were not autistic, they were blind!*

I turned to the director of the school. He must have seen the shock in my face. He put his arm around my shoulders and said, "Dr. Delacato, I know what you're thinking. You're wondering what the children are doing with all those repetitive motions. We who work with the blind are very familiar with these behaviors. Most blind children have them. *They are called blindisms.*"

I was astounded. What were called *autisms* in the psychological world were called *blindisms* in the world of the blind!

One of my final visits was to a school for the deaf. It was a fateful day. I didn't want to go. What could deaf children teach me? I walked into the school for the deaf. I was late. They were in the midst of a silent prayer. It was the noisiest silent prayer I had ever seen or heard! I sat in the back of the large room. I saw heads bobbing, gently hitting the chair in front of them. I saw children gently, or not so gently, hitting themselves on the ear. I heard strange rhythmic vocal noises. All of these in that same rhythm—the rhythm of the *autisms!*

Again I was shocked. These children were *not* autistic. They were deaf. *Yet they had the same behavior!*

After the prayer, the director came back to welcome me. We talked for a long time. I carefully skirted around the subject of the behavior I had observed.

They were autisms, I knew, but how would I ask? As we talked, I finally decided to ask about rhythmic behavior. The director said, "Of course, Dr. Delacato, our children have rhythmic behavior. Most deaf children do. *We call them deafisms.*"

Autisms, blindisms, deafisms! They all looked the same —the same rhythm. *Could they all be the same thing?*

What did the "blindisms" and "deafisms" have in common? They both represent sensory problems, or ways in which we perceive the world through the eyes and the ears. We could call them "sensoryisms."

Now I had to see many more blind children to see what their "blindisms" had in common. The blindisms consisted of head-rocking, moving a hand or object in front of the face in bright light, especially in sunlight, incessantly spinning an object held in the hand, or rhythmically poking at the side of one or both eyes. All of these behaviors had something to do with vision—or the eye/brain relationship!

When I went back to the deaf children, I quickly saw the same relationship. All of their "deafisms" had something to do with sound and hearing. They banged things rhythmically, made rhythmic vocal sounds, or tapped or tore things rhythmically—all related to hearing! Here again, the child's behavior is definitely related to his sensory problem.

And now the question became more obvious.

Could it be that such behaviors—whether we call them autisms, deafisms, or blindisms—are all related to a sensory channel problem?

Could it be that autisms were the same thing, but that we forgave the blind and deaf children *because* they were blind or deaf?

When a child is brain-injured, he has a perceptual problem—which means he is a *little blind* and a *little deaf*. Could it be that autistic children were brain-injured?

I went back to the original article of Kanner's. I read over the symptoms given for each child in the article. Many are what today are considered *"soft signs"* of brain injury. With today's knowledge would they be considered brain-injured?

Perhaps, at last, this wasn't a dead end. If children who were mildly or moderately brain-injured had problems taking in the stimulation from the world to their brains, what would they do?

Would they repeatedly stimulate themselves in an effort to cure themselves? If this were true, I could break the code! Was autistic children's alien behavior in reality their attempt to cure themselves? Were they trying to open up or normalize one or more of the five channels from the world to their brains?

Were they like the tiny silvery fish of the Araguaya—was their strange behavior a desperate attempt at survival or a desperate attempt at self-treatment of a severe sensory problem?

If so, the autistic child is telling us he has a sensory problem. We only have to watch him and, if his autisms fall into a category (such as sounds), then the sensory problem he is telling us about is his hearing. If his autisms all involve vision, then it is his vision he is telling us about.

There are five channels into the brain: seeing, hearing, tasting, smelling, and feeling through the skin.

I would never again call these behaviors—the need for which stole the child's attention away from us—"autisms." In the future I would call them deafisms, blindisms, taste-isms, smellisms, or tactilisms.

I now knew *how* to see or hear the message. I was no longer blind or deaf to the constant and desperate cry for help of these children.

I would watch their behavior. Why were they stimulating one of the five channels into the brain repeatedly—their eyes, their ears, their nose, their mouth, or their skin?

Their behavior now told me where they needed help.

But I needed more proof.

If autisms were a reflection of sensory problems, perhaps we could create them simply by giving someone a severe enough sensory problem. Since it was not proper to do so with children, I decided to do so with an animal. Because light and dark are so completely controlled by a turtle as he ejects or withdraws his head from his shell, I decided to see if I could cause visualisms with a turtle.

I placed the turtle in a six-by-nine-foot cage in which he had total freedom of movement. I gave him ample food and plenty of light. Following a two-week adjustment period, in which he could become accustomed to a cage and the placement of food and water, I taped both of his eyes shut with electrical tape.

For the first four days the turtle wandered about the cage, aimlessly trying to find an opening in the cage wall. He ate and drank from the containers. Beginning on the fifth day, and increasing with time, the turtle periodically sat with his head and neck extending as far out of his shell as possible—swinging his head in the air from side to side —in seemingly meaningless repetitive motion. He had developed a visualism! This behavior continued for another week, at which time I removed the tape from his eyes. This "autistic" behavior persisted for a day and a half, and then disappeared.

The turtle was very active, almost hyperactive, during his first three days of renewed sight, but after that time his activity returned to normal.

At no time did he revert to repetitive head movement!

I had been able to cause an autism and to get rid of it through changing one sensory channel.

Now a pattern began to form. I saw many children and listed their "isms." When I found which channel or channels into the brain were affected, I gave an outsized amount of stimulation to that channel.

I returned to Nancy. Since the swelling from the car door injury had gone, the skin was no longer black and blue and now she was biting again. She had reverted to her old practice of biting her hand!

I could only conclude that she was trying to make her hand hurt! She was trying to open a channel between her hand and her brain! She was treating herself!

Now it was clear. We took her hand, immersed it in ice water, then hot water, pinched it, brushed it, even rubbed it with rough sandpaper and coarse towels. And the hand-biting stopped! Nancy no longer needed to treat herself by trying to normalize the nerve channels between her hand and brain. We did it *for* her, through stimulation, and her biting stopped.

Now I had made a start in understanding these behaviors. *These children were not psychotic. They were brain-injured and had severe sensory problems. They could not deal with the stimulation coming into their brains from the outside world. One or more of their intake channels (sight, sound, taste, smell, or feel) was deficient in some way. Their strange repetitive behavior was their attempt, through much repetitive stimulation, to normalize that channel or channels.*

These children were not autistic for psychological reasons; they behaved as they did for neurological reasons. They were brain-injured.

I had finally broken at least part of the code!

V
"TO TELL OR NOT TO TELL"

An exciting idea—a possible new way to help children—
the thrill of discovery! I should have been elated, but I
wasn't.

The idea was too different. It was too much of a de-
parture from all that had gone before. It would upset all
those who had spent their lives looking at these children
psychologically instead of perceptually and neurologically.

Maybe it was just a far-out, wild idea. If so, it would
be ignored. But if it turned out to be true and useful, it
would lead to more attacks. If it proved true, it could not
be ignored, and this meant more trouble for me, the
Domans, and most importantly, the Institutes.

Even if it were a valid idea, I had no proof that sensoryisms could be changed through treatment. This would be
the place to start. Could we decrease the sensoryisms? Was
it possible? Could we eliminate the sensoryisms through
treatment? We had to experiment.

We took every child who came to us for the first time
between March 1, 1967 and May 30, 1967 who met the
following criteria:

had a previous diagnosis of autism and/or early childhood
schizophrenia made by some outside authority;
received a diagnosis by us of brain injury, and had at least
one year of our treatment.

There were ten children who met these criteria. We inter-
viewed each set of parents relative to the absence or presence of the following sensoryisms:

rocking
repetitive and nongoal-directed eating
    "   "   "   " drinking
    "   "   "   " speech
body twirling
object banging
finger play
play in front of eyes
tactilisms
arm flailing
total withdrawal
tasteisms
smellisms
inappropriate laughing
paper shredding
highly selective eating

We asked each parent to rate his child's sensory behavior
for the beginning of treatment and after a year of treatment
on the following scale:

0   none at all
1   very slight
2   moderate amount
3   most of the time

Using this scale we gave each child "before" and "after" sensoryism scores. Each of the ten children showed a decrease in the sensoryism scores. Percent of decrease ranged from 92 percent to 32 percent, with a median decrease of 56 percent in sensoryism scores on this interview scale.[1]

Now that I knew that sensoryisms could be changed, I was ready for the next step.

I had to try out the idea on knowledgeable people. I had to show them some children so they could understand. The most knowledgeable people I could choose were the mothers of autistic children. I took one mother and her child at a time, explained the theory, and then both the child's mother and I watched the child. I asked each mother to pick out the sensory inputs she thought her child was seeking through his strange, nongoal-directed and repetitive behavior.

"Your child is attempting to normalize one of the five channels into his brain through repetitive stimulation of that channel (taste, smell, vision, hearing, or feeling). If we can ascertain which one of the channels is affected, we can break his behavior code. We can find ways of normalizing the channel. If we normalize it, the behavior should disappear. But first we must watch him and break the code."

I shall always be grateful to those courageous mothers who sat with me, shared their fears, and then proceeded to teach me so much. When they understood the theory, they expanded on it with all kinds of examples, additions, and clarification from their experiences with their own children. I was being taught by the "real" experts—the mother of each autistic child.

They invited me into their homes. I looked into every

---

[1] With grateful appreciation to Barbara Hardy and Frank Dickson, who carried out the interviews and arrived at the scores.

corner of their lives to see if there were psychological factors that I was missing. They were just like all families with their weaknesses, strengths, and problems. Nowhere could I find any indication of rejection, deep psychological problems, or lack of love. What I did find was sadness, lack of hope, and frustration—all caused by the strange behavior of their autistic child.

These were happy days. These mothers taught me. Their families sensed that we were doing something different. Even the autistic children seemed increasingly more able to accept me.

What we had formerly termed "autisms" disappeared. What I now saw were sensoryisms. My whole attitude had changed. I began to devise treatment techniques.

With the new knowledge that the mothers gave me, and with a greater sense of security in the idea, I decided to try it on Dart.

He always sat on my side of the desk so that he could look at each child's chart with me. He had spent thirty years of his life with the medical Establishment and its conservative approach to new ideas, but he had been an innovator. His new ideas had created a great deal of criticism. It had affected his life in many ways, both positive and negative. I decided to move slowly.

"Dr. Dart, when you finally cleared away all the limestone from that first fateful skull, what did you think?"

"Carl, no one has ever asked me that question during the almost fifty years since that incident. Let's see if I can answer it.

"I knew from the outset that this brain was too big to belong in this part of the world. Here was what seemed an anthropoid brain living in the temperate zone. The blast at the limestone quarry had freed the brain from the stone above, and now I was digging the limestone away from the face to see if it corresponded to the brain. Would the face carry the same message as the brain? And it did, even though it was the brain and face of a child.

"It wasn't a shocking conclusion to me, probably because the process of cleaning the limestone away from the face was so gradual and so slow. You must recall that it was the first time I had ever dug out a fossil, so I had to do it with exceeding care. I used my wife's knitting needles, and it took almost three months of daily work.

"This gradual clearing away of the limestone led me gradually to come closer to my conclusion. Each day's work led me one day closer to the conclusion. So you see, it wasn't a sudden thing. As the face unfolded, my conclusion unfolded."

He hadn't drawn his great conclusion as a sudden strike of insight! Instead, it was a gradual unfolding as he peeled away the limestone and found that the message of the brain was corroborated by the characteristics of the face. I was reassured. I asked another question. "When you were really convinced that it was a man-ape skull, did you suspect the reaction your announcement might cause?"

"I knew that there would be a great reaction, both positive and negative. Remember, Carl, when we talk about our own origins there are bound to be strong feelings.

"Everybody was so convinced that everything had come from the east to the west, like the daily sunlight. I knew also that there would be the greatest psychological resistance from Europeans to any enlightenment that came from the southern part of Africa.

"But I knew, and so did they, that Darwin had predicted that Africa would probably prove to have been the cradle of mankind, and yet the presence of anthropoids or hominids that had succeeded in adapting to a hunting life in the open territory of the temperate zone of this vast continent was something that could not have entered even Darwin's imagination during the last century."

Now I would come closer to my problem. "Did you ever consider not writing the article announcing your findings?"

"Oh, not for a minute!"

His blue eyes twinkled, he smiled, and he walked over to my large window and looked out over my lush valley. I wondered about his thoughts fifty years ago as he viewed so many other valleys with exotic names, such as Sterkfontein, Makapan, and Taungs. I had been to those valleys with him. Some had called those valleys the Garden of Eden, where man was born. I was always in awe in those valleys. But what was Dart thinking now?

"Carl, you have something on your mind. Come out with it!"

I had no choice now. I had to try my new theory on him.

I went through what I had done, what I had found, and now my idea:

"Sir, the world has been looking at these problems psychologically. They are wrong. These are *neurological* problems. Furthermore, the child's behavior tells us where the problem lies. When we know where the problem is, we can begin to treat it."

Dart had listened attentively. Now he stood up and looked out the window again into the valley for a long time. He turned toward me and quietly said, "Carl, you must refine your idea, keeping careful records and, when you are ready, you have a responsibility to tell the world."

The mothers had understood, and now Dart wasn't shocked. But they both represented biased groups. I had to try out the idea on somebody who knew the *field* and someone who didn't know *me*. If this kind of person didn't laugh or tell me that it was a crazy idea, then I would tell Glenn and Bob.

How long would the Institutes tolerate the attacks that my ideas created? Glenn would be a good barometer. If he paled when I told him, I would know that he foresaw more trouble for the Institutes. If he laughed, or told me it was a crazy idea, I would go on, but if he paled I would know he was worried about the Institutes. Then I would have a problem.

The drive from Munich to Seewiesen, with the snow-covered Alps looming in the distance, was picturesque and restful. I told Glenn I would drive and he could relax and enjoy the Alpine scenery.

In a few hours we would meet Konrad Lorenz at the Max Planck Institute. Glenn and I had received awards from the International Forum for Human Potential and, as former recipients, we were commissioned to deliver this year's award to Konrad Lorenz.

The award was given to Lorenz for his "pioneering work in the physiology of behavior, such as the trigger mechanism of aggression, the rituals devised to control the destructiveness of aggression, his delineation of the early imprinting phenomenon as a basis of learning."

It would be a great honor to meet Konrad Lorenz. He, Ardrey, Morris, and Dart were the world's leaders in ethology. Lorenz had written *King Solomon's Ring, On Aggression,* and *Man Meets Dog.* Meeting Lorenz would complete the circle. He was the last of the great triumvirate. Lorenz had been trained as a psychiatrist. Now he ran the Max Planck Institutes in Seewiesen, where he continued his research on the behavior of tropical fish and the Graylag geese.

Driving through the picture-book villages in the sparkling sunshine, I thought back to Max Planck. This great scientist had once said:

It is one of the most painful experiences of my entire scientific career that I have seldom—in fact, I might say never—succeeded in obtaining universal recognition for a new result, the truth of which I could demonstrate by a conclusive but only theoretical proof. . . . A new scientific truth does not triumph by convincing its opponents and making them see the light; but it triumphs because its opponents finally die off, leaving a new generation that is familiar with the new idea.

On the outskirts of quiet and peaceful snow-covered Seewiesen was the Max Planck Institute. Konrad Lorenz was expecting us. He met us with great warmth, and his English was much better than I had expected. He was a much taller man than I had imagined. His flowing white hair, his ruddy complexion, and his ease of movement gave the impression of a man comfortable in the outdoors.

His warmth and friendliness made us feel very much at home. He apologized for the fact that his wife was not home to meet us.

He led us through the research areas of the Institute with pride. After our tour he tentatively asked, "Would you like to come along to feed the geese?"

Glenn and I answered simultaneously, "We thought you would never ask." He looked down at our feet and said, "You are both wearing good shoes for the trip. Come, here is a bucket for each of you."

We stopped on the way out to the hillside pasture and filled our buckets with grain for the Graylag geese, who were nowhere in sight. The top of the snow was melting in the warm sunshine as we walked through a field toward the foothill pasture. At the top of the hill we stopped.

Konrad Lorenz began making noises that sounded remarkably like duck calls. As he continued, geese began to circle the horizon and gradually circled closer, in a reconnaissance maneuver to be sure that Glenn and I were safe to be near. When they decided we were safe, they began to land. There were almost one hundred of them.

These were obviously Lorenz's friends. Many of the geese came up to him as if to say hello. A few made aggressive passes at us as they walked toward the grain we threw on the ground.

Lorenz talked about his geese lovingly. He had names for each one of them, and he recognized each as a separate personality. It was fascinating to listen to this great man who had learned so much about aggression and instinct from watching and studying these wild geese. There were a few Mallard ducks among the geese. Lorenz explained that, through being with the geese as babies they had become imprinted as geese, not ducks. They now thought they *were* geese. We talked about his imprint theories and how they affect learning.

And now it was time for the geese to leave. Each Graylag has to go through a thorough preparation to take off. He wiggles his body and moves his head back and forth, almost as if he were a pilot checking the controls, before he takes off. If this process is interrupted he can't take off. Instead, he starts all over again, going through his complete readying ritual before taking off.

"Come, I will feed you some German soup for lunch."

Although reluctant to leave this high pasture, where so much of man's understanding of his own aggressions and learning started, we followed Lorenz to his home because we were very hungry.

As we followed Lorenz, Glenn and I agreed that before lunch would be a good time to present the award that we had come all the way from Philadelphia to Seewiesen to present to Lorenz.

I had seen this award presented in the most opulent surroundings, with five simultaneous translations going on, surrounded by men in formal clothes and women in long dresses, all being filmed by movie and television cameras, but I had never seen such a beautiful reception of the award (a statuette of a child walking) as on this occasion.

Glenn and I stood by the grand piano in Konrad Lorenz's living room, with the sun streaming in the large windows, and we made the presentation. Lorenz looked at the statue as we presented it to him. He lifted it, looked at it carefully, and then placed it on the piano. He was obviously touched.

There were only three of us in the room. He thanked us genuinely and warmly. He had just received an honorary Doctor of Science degree from Yale University and now this second honor. He was very moved and made a gracious speech. As he spoke, I was saddened that there were not the hundreds of others who admired his work, here to hear him. It was a noble and inspired speech with an urgent hope for mankind.

The soup was full of large beef chunks and cabbage chunks. We chatted about our families, our work.

"Tell me what you are doing that is new at the Institutes these days," Lorenz asked.

Glenn looked up and said, "Carl's doing some exciting things in behavior. Carl, tell him about your activities."

This was it! This great man whose work had been in the field of behavior, whose international reputation for teaching man about his own instincts, was sitting across a soup plate from me, and now I had to tell him.

I talked slowly and carefully, going through my search for the "autisms" and finding "blindisms" and "deafisms." I explained that I felt *autisms* were *sensoryisms* and were indications of brain injury. They were not indications of psychosis but of brain injury, which interfered with one of the five channels into the brain from the outside world.

I watched him carefully as I talked. Since he was our host, he would be polite, but could I detect something in his manner? He smiled and nodded his head throughout my talk. He did not touch his soup.

When I had finished, he looked at me thoughtfully. "This is an interesting new idea—I shall be interested in your further findings."

He hadn't laughed, he hadn't resisted. I looked at him in great relief.

In my eagerness to tell Lorenz about my findings, I had forgotten that Glenn was also listening to my theory for the first time. What had he thought? I had been so intent on Lorenz's reaction that I hadn't watched for Glenn's. My reverie was broken.

"Carl, have more soup. You've never eaten soup like this in the States," said Glenn as he ladled some soup into my plate.

And now I could work on—Lorenz wasn't shocked, he even seemed interested in my idea, and Glenn hadn't paled. In fact, he had passed the soup!

We spent the next few hours talking about behavior. The sun sank down behind the hills, and now the room was no longer bathed in sunshine. We stood up to leave.

"We've taken too much of your time."

"Would you like to come back up on the hill to feed the geese again before you go?" I was now completely convinced. He was not upset with my theory.

We learned more about instinct, aggression, and imprinting on that hill than I had learned in all the hours I had spent reading. The geese were becoming individual personalities to us, too.

We were all sad as we said goodbye. Glenn and I had met a great man.

The drive back to Munich was restful and delightful. I was relaxed. Now I was in a hurry to go home. There were many unanswered questions to be looked into. There were many children to be seen.

VI
TOO MUCH, TOO LITTLE, OR WHITE NOISE?

Now was the time to put the theory to the test in every way possible. There were many children to be seen. They all seemed to fall into a pattern of sensory problems. I wrote a description of "isms" I saw, and each fit into the theory very well. But there was something missing. I could not seem to predict each child's reaction.

For example, a number of my children had bathroom problems. This concerned me because those who had theorized previously from a psychoanalytical point of view, had pointed out that autistic children had difficulty with bathrooms. Those theorists related the bathroom problems to how rigidly their mothers had attempted to toilet train the children. They felt that the children's lack of cooperation in the bathroom was a form of getting back at the mothers. Another theory was that the child was acquisitive and wouldn't let go of his feces because it would be letting go of part of himself that was already lacking.

But these theories fell short. The bathroom problems were more complex. About half of the autistic children loved to play and be in the bathroom, and the other half screamed hysterically whenever we attempted to get them into a bathroom.

Their bathroom performance was also split up. One group would not defecate and was obviously "holding it in," while the other happily defecated and even painted their feces over themselves or on the walls. Why the differences?

Many of the children arrived with a diagnosis of deafness. Some of these "deaf" children loved to sit next to a dishwasher or washing machine for hours on end, listening to its motor. Others of these "deaf" children shrieked and covered their ears to drown out the sounds of such things as the kitchen electric mixer or a lawn mower. Although both were labeled "deaf," their reactions to sounds were extremely different.

Still others would sit quietly, as though listening to some inner voice. These children acted as though there were something inside themselves that they were listening to, with rapt attention. Periodically they would scream for no apparent reason.

My observations were made more difficult by the fact that all of these children had "deafisms." Why, if they all had problems with their hearing channels, did they react so differently?

I saw a number of self-mutilating and self-manipulating children. When tested, they fell into two groups: those whom you couldn't touch because their skins were too sensitive, and those who smiled only when you pricked their skin with a pin until the blood came.

There were some children who vacantly stared at the world about them through very dilated eyes, and there were those who examined every minute particle of dust they could find. There were those who seemed to be very carefully studying something that was not there. All three of these groups fell into the category of having repetitive behavior that dealt with vision. Why, then, were their reactions so different?

As I saw more children and categorized their "isms," they began to fall into a pattern.

One group of children was *hyper* in its sensory systems. It was as though the brain injury had caused a seeming short-circuit in their sensory systems, and the least bit of input would activate the system. As a result, these children felt, smelled, tasted, heard, or saw *too well!*

These were the children who covered their ears with the slightest noise, who were upset by even the slightest smells, to whom a touch or tickle of their skin appeared painful, whose taste was too effective so that they wouldn't eat many things, and whose eyes were too sensitive.

These children did many things in order to survive. Normal surroundings such as sounds, sights, smells, tastes, or feels were painful to them. These children have great difficulty surviving in a normal world because they cannot handle the amount of stimulation to certain senses coming in to them. It is too much.

It is also too different. One child cried in pain and covered his ears every time I turned on the fluorescent lights in my office. He heard a high-pitched noise coming from the light that none of us with normal hearing could hear. In order to survive in the world, these children had learned to "turn off" the sounds of the world. Otherwise they were in constant pain from the world of stimulation.

What had confused me was that these children *did not react* in the same way *to the noise that they made themselves*. These children were quite noisy in their "isms" and their attempts to treat themselves.

When the noise came from a source other than themselves, they reacted with fear and withdrawal.

To help these auditory children survive their fears for the moment, I plugged up their ears with wax. Their behavior changed dramatically. They no longer ran from the bathroom or loud engines. We had taken a very small preliminary step in helping them to survive in our world's level of stimulation.

Their nervous systems had hair triggers in some areas of intake. A tiny stimulus set off a dramatic reaction in their "hyper" nervous systems. It seemed that they had large, eight-lane super highways from their sensory organs to their brains. The message reached there faster and stronger than expected.

The second group that fell into a pattern was the group that had sensory channels that were *hypo*. *These children had channels that didn't allow enough information to get to the brain.* They needed greater stimulation to get through. These were the children with poor smell, who ate indiscriminately. Some of them loved to smell their own feces. These kinds of children loved the bathroom because sound reverberated around the room, bouncing off the shiny porcelain surfaces and tile walls. They loved the noises made by the kitchen appliances. They smiled when spanked or pinched. It seemed as though the channel between their sense organs and brain was clogged or underdeveloped.

They needed more stimulation to get through the channel to their brain. It seemed as though they had small, winding roads from their sense organs to their brains.

The third group, or type, had internal sensory interference that decreased their sensory system's ability to deal with the world. I called this interference "white noise."

If you turn on a radio, it makes a hum. When you turn

the dial to a station that is broadcasting, you no longer hear the hum, you listen to the broadcast. The same is true for an amplifying system. When you first turn it on, you hear the hum (white noise), but when you start talking over the system, you no longer hear the hum. Your brain cuts it out, but theirs cannot. They continue to hear the hum or white noise.

With the "white noise" children the noise-within-the-system interferes with the sensory system's efficiency. For example, children who have white noise in the taste system always have a taste in their mouths. When they taste something, the constant taste they have in their mouths (white noise) interferes with their tasting the food they are eating.

Some children who have auditory white noise hear their own hearts beating, their digestion progressing, and can hear their circulation, especially near their ears. These system noises interfere with their hearing the sounds coming from the world about them.

Let's take an example of white noise in the feeling, or tactility area, and see its effect. Children who have tactile "white noise" often feel that they have something touching their skin when there really is nothing touching their skin. They quite often "itch" for no apparent reason. As a result, the system's internal noise interferes with the system's operation and perception.

This was the second part of the code that was now broken. The repetitive behavior, which stole our children's attention, could be placed in one or more of five sensory channels. The problems with these channels fell into one of three categories:

1. *Hyper:* a hair-trigger sensory system that allowed *too much* of the sensory message into the brain.

2. *Hypo:* a sluggish sensory system that allowed *too little* of the sensory message into the brain.
3. *White noise:* a sensory system that operated so inefficiently that its own operation created an *interference* or *noise* in the system.

As we began treating our newly categorized "sensoryisms," we found that after we helped the child to "survive," treatment could be directed at "normalizing" the channel. This meant that, after the initial "survival" or "first aid" techniques, we could treat all the children in the same way. We gave them sensory stimulation in the frequency, intensity, and duration that they could handle comfortably. As they gained more experience, using a particular sensory channel successfully, it gradually normalized. As it did, the need for the repetitive behavior disappeared, and the child could now pay attention to and join our world.

Our research with primitive tribes continued. We were continuing to find that children who were not allowed to crawl and creep before they walked did not fully develop their nervous systems.

In two days we would leave the Brazilian jungle and return to civilization. The evening was warm, but the Xingu River was clear and cool. The Xingu Indians were enjoying the coolness of the water. Whole families frolicked in the water. As we dove in, the women all left the water. They were embarrassed to be seen bathing. They stood, naked, on the bank and watched us. There was no modesty attached to their leaving the river because no one in the tribe ever wore any clothing. Our mutual nakedness was of no concern. The women stood on the bank and giggled at us as we now frolicked in the river.

Veras swam over to me and said, "Carl, it is our last

night. Come, we must cook a delicious dinner for our Indian friends. We have fish, beans, and rice."

The mosquitos were beginning to bite as Veras and I argued about how to prepare the fish stew. We always disagreed about food. We chopped off the fish heads and scaled the fish for the stew. Since we had no vegetables, I went across the clearing and picked a few limes and cut some young palmetto branches.

Veras shook his head in disapproval as he watched me peel off the palmetto bark and cut the white pulp into the stew. I noticed that everything in our stew was white. I wished I had something colorful to throw into the pot. Veras threw more wood on the fire and sat down.

"Carl, how does the research go with the autistic children?"

My answer was interrupted by Bob, who brought each of us a shirt. "Here are your pills." It was our daily dose of an antimalarial drug.

"Bob, come and sit. Carl was just going to tell me about his research and his new ideas. I hope they are better than his stew," Veras persevered.

I sat across the fire from them and told them both the entire story. They listened attentively, except for Veras, occasionally stirring the fish and rice stew, disapprovingly, and the now-boiling pot of black beans, of which he seemed to approve.

Bob looked at me thoughtfully. "Carl, I'm intrigued. I don't agree with some of your ideas, but your approach makes sense; write it up as quickly as possible."

I was relieved.

Veras remained silent. I stirred the fish and rice, squeezed a few more limes into the mixture, and Veras stirred the black beans.

"Raymundo, why are you so silent?"

He picked up the large pot of black beans, smiled his Buddha-like smile, and answered, "Carl, bring the stew. Our guests are waiting."

I was puzzled as I ladled out the white stew to our appreciative and smiling naked guests. Veras didn't talk. He just covered each serving of stew with a heaping serving of black beans, almost as if he were deliberately trying to hide my stew.

São Paulo is the largest Brazilian city. Although not nearly as endowed with Old World charm as Rio de Janeiro, or as starkly representative of the twentieth century as Brasilia, which we had just left, it is the scientific and industrial hub of Brazil.

The coat and tie felt restrictive and unfamiliar to me as we stood in the receiving line greeting the distinguished physicians, therapists, and professors from Brazil, Argentina, and Peru. Summer evenings in São Paulo are pleasant. The endless traffic jams finally unravel and the Brazilians become themselves—charming, urbane, and soft.

The sumptuous dinner, the elegant surroundings, the erudite conversations, all made our white fish stew of twenty-four hours ago seem unreal and far away.

As we were served our tiny cups of pungent Brazilian coffee, Veras rose. He announced that there would be translation of his remarks into English in deference to the North American guests. He made introductory remarks in Portuguese and then the translator said, "I have surprise for you. Two days ago, in the heart of the Xingu, I heard a new and important idea about children. Tonight we, in Brazil, will have the honor to hear that idea for the first time. Indeed, it is the first time the idea has been presented publicly. I will translate."

I started my impromptu presentation by describing the

day that Veras had pressured me into going into the area of behavior. I thanked him at length for his support and encouragement. I meant it, but I knew that he edited most of my thanks out of his translation into Portuguese. He translated my presentation with obvious pride. As I finished, he embraced me in the typical Brazilian *abraço* and whispered in English, "Your theory is better than your fish stew."

It takes a little more than an hour to fly from São Paulo to Rio de Janeiro. Veras sat next to me pointing out familiar landmarks. His physician son sat across the aisle. Veras was proud of his nation.

"Carl, I like your new theory."

We were approaching the mountains that surround Rio.

"Raymundo, I have only one real worry. Even with this theory, I am failing some children. Is it right to offer a new approach that may not work for all children? Is it right to raise false hope?"

Veras turned toward me. His face was just six inches from mine. He spoke slowly, in a somewhat too-loud whisper.

"Carl, there is no such thing as *false* hope, just as there are no *false* dreams. No, without hope there is no progress."

The stewardess interrupted him, insisting that he fasten his seat belt. We were in the approach pattern for Rio. I could see the overpowering statue of Christ on the mountain.

"Look, Carl, there on the mountain, it is the Christ. He is our symbol. His outstretched arms are the daily symbol of *hope* for all our people—of all religions. Every time hope is not fulfilled, should we take our Christ down from the mountain? Carl, we all need hope. These children and their parents need hope. There is no such thing as *false* hope. There is only the failure to reach our hopes. That is why we have tomorrows; they are another chance to reach our hopes."

We landed. He smiled as he discovered that he had forgotten to fasten his seat belt. His son leaned across the aisle and said, "Come, you two, stop talking. We have children to see."

Veras was always eloquent and always convincing.

VII
THE PUZZLE FITS

With this new piece of the puzzle my new theory now became clearer:

1. Autistic children are not psychotic. They are brain-injured.
2. Brain injury causes perceptual dysfunction, that is, it causes some problem with one or more of the channels from the world to the brain—seeing, hearing, tasting, feeling, or smelling.
3. These channels are made abnormal by the brain injury in one of the following ways:

   Hyper: The channel is too open and, as a result, too much stimulation gets in for the brain to handle comfortably.

   Hypo: The channel is not open enough and, as a result, too little of the stimulation gets in and the brain is deprived.

   White noise: The channel creates its own stimulus because of its faulty operation and, as a result, the message from the outside world is garbled or, in extreme cases, is overcome by the noise in the system.

4. The repetitive strange behaviors of the autistic child, *which are called autisms,* are *symptoms* of brain injury.

5. These repetitive behaviors *should not* be called autisms because they are *sensoryisms.* These repetitive sensoryisms are the child's attempts to normalize the affected sensory channels.

6. The child is attempting to treat himself.

7. It is this attempt to treat himself and to normalize his sensory channels that steals the child's attention away from reality. It also keeps him from *surviving* in the real world.

8. This behavior is the child's message. All we have to do is observe it and it tells us which channels are affected.

9. By closely observing the child's behavior we can learn:

    a. which sensory channel is not normal.
    b. whether the channel is hyper, hypo, or white noise.

10. When we have learned which channels are affected, we can help the child to normalize the channels by giving him the proper experience and stimulation through that channel.

11. As the channel is normalized, the strange repetitive behavior ceases.

12. When the strange repetitive behavior ceases, the child's attention is shifted and he becomes able to learn to deal with the real world and to learn and to interact with things and people about him.

13. At that point we treat him as we would treat any other mildly to moderately brain-injured children we see, and he can now profit from the treatment.

But theories must have practical applications. There are three goals that have to be met:

1. Understanding the alien behavior as symptoms.
2. Providing, at the outset, a survival environment to deal with the behavioral symptoms.

3. Instituting treatment aimed at the *cause* of the problem.

Since these symptoms were so strange and since they took the form of behavior, it was difficult to understand them. In addition, dealing *only* with the symptoms would help the child survive for the moment, but in the end we would have to deal with the cause: the brain injury.

We could only deal with the cause after we had changed the symptoms enough to help the child to survive. We had to achieve the first two goals rapidly. Then we would move on to treat the basic cause.

With these criteria in mind, re-examine the cases of Bobby, Ann, Jerry, Andy, and Susan at the beginning of Chapter II. See how well you can diagnose and understand their seemingly meaningless behavior as symptoms.

Bobby (page 16) looked right through me as he moved around the room, constantly waving his hand in front of his face. Why? Could it be that he was gently moving air toward his nose, constantly monitoring the smell in the air and in the room?

He was intrigued by smoke, which has an odor. When he sat ten feet away from me, he felt safe from my smells, and then I did the terrible thing. I blew my waste-laden and smoke-scented breath at him. It was the smell of my breath that made him nauseous and caused him to vomit on my rug. My breath blew very close to his parents but they weren't affected because their smell systems were normal, not *hyper,* as was Bobby's.

Can you imagine the difficulty trying to hug or to caress Bobby? He won't allow anyone that close to him because, to him, *we smell.*

Can you imagine how Bobby suffers when the house is full of strong cooking odors? Can you understand why

Bobby would fight at the breast? The pungent odor of the nipple and the increased perspiration of his mother while nursing him surrounded him with insurmountable odors.

We had to start treating Bobby by giving him a relatively odor-free environment that would not upset him and would not force him to live with overpowering and uncomfortable smells. We then began to give him gentle experiences with smell. We told him what we were going to have him smell, then moved the material near him. He began to learn to separate and differentiate smells. He began to learn to tolerate them. It took us six months to work up to strong odors of vinegar and mustard.

While working with his smell experiences, we also added taste. His appetite increased and, as he made progress, he was able to move closer to us as people, tolerating the smell that each of us exudes. He is now able to sit next to another person and does so in his daily tutoring sessions.

Re-evaluate Ann (page 17), who wore the football helmet because she banged herself on the head constantly.

Let's assume Ann heard a constant and painful ringing noise in her head. What would she do to change the noise? If this auditory white noise were loud enough, it drowned out all sounds coming from the outside and could be very painful coming from the inside. When she banged her head, the noise stopped for a bit.

In order to help Ann to learn to suppress these internal noises, we rolled her on the floor, we stood her on her head, and we spun her until she was dizzy. Each of these activities made the sound that she heard inside her head different. We gave her an electronic stethoscope so that she could spend a great deal of time listening to each part of her body at rest and when quiet. She began to learn about her body noises and she began to listen to us as we whispered to her. As her head banging decreased she became able to survive. We began to treat her as we would any moderately brain-injured child. At the last visit for re-evaluation, her mother reported that Ann now goes outdoors to ride bicycles with the neighborhood children—without wearing a helmet or even a hat.

Jerry (page 18) had lived all of his life in constant fear of sound. Loud noises, when made by others, sent him into a rage or into frightened hysterics. His method of survival was to act deaf to the sounds made by others, and to make his own series of noises for himself.

My whistle was a very upsetting and piercing sound. It followed an automobile ride through noisy traffic, an interval in a noisy waiting room filled with many people talking, and being surrounded by new, unpredictable, and frightening sounds. My loud noise caused his hysterics.

In order to help him to survive, before we initiated treatment, we blocked his ears with sterile wax. Thus, sound was not allowed into his auditory system. This immediately changed Jerry's behavior. For the moment, at least, he could survive. We instituted our treatment for a moderately brain-injured child, and Jerry can now play happily with other children. We have not yet succeeded completely, for Jerry still wears special earplugs that contain a small valve. When the noise around Jerry is too loud, the vibrations of the noise close the valve, which blocks out the loud sounds. We can converse with Jerry, but the conversation always goes better if we are in a quiet room and talk in a quiet voice.

Andy (page 19) was hypo in smell. Since he did not perceive at his brain enough of the message about smell, he worked hard at giving the world a smell that he recognized and knew—that of his own urine.

We are surrounding Andy with strong and recognizable smells. He can now discriminate one smell from another.

We give him strong smells—vinegar, gasoline, mustard, and so forth—in isolation from other smells. He enjoys strong smells and cooperates. He no longer needs to give everything in a room his own smell. The attention that the smell "ism" had stolen from us is now being focused on our developmental program.

Susan (page 20) was hypo in tactility. Not enough of the tactile message from the skin arrived at her brain. Her biting of her hands was her attempt at normalizing the channel from her hand to her brain.

Susan no longer bites. She no longer needs to bite. We have normalized for her the channel between her hand and her brain. We brushed, rubbed, hit, massaged, and pinched her hands. We submerged them in hot water, then in ice water. We placed itching and mildly irritating solutions on her hands. Also, we lightly sanded her hands with coarse sandpaper. We gave her hands and arms deep, almost painful, massage.

Susan doesn't bite her hands any longer, for one simple reason. If she bit her hand now, "it would hurt," she says proudly.

Being able to understand strange behavioral symptoms and being able to change them enough so that the child reached a survival level meant that the child was no longer considered a candidate for residential institutionalization.

Happily, these children could now be treated as straightforward problems of brain injury, with which I had much experience. Even more happily, as a group they responded to treatment quite well. An additional bonus was the fact that they were, in general, *not* severely brain-injured but were, instead, mild or moderate. There was an additional bonus, which gradually became more evident. These children had *learned to pay attention* during their presurvival period. True, they paid attention to strange sensory inputs and they paid such attention to those that they could not survive in our real world. Once freed from the yoke of having to pay attention to their own strange sensory problems, they could pay attention as we wanted them to. They were able to pay attention to our work, especially in reading, writing, and arithmetic; and they made good progress.

VIII
READING THE SENSORYISMS

Listening to a symphony or watching a ballet can be a moving experience in communication, but watching an autistic child's movements can be a much more thrilling experience in communication; for within each ritualistic movement is contained a frightened cry for help, for understanding.

The first rule is: Don't be frightened. Sit back and enjoy this symphony of movement. Remember that the child is both orchestra and dancer. And above all, he is the composer and the choreographer—desperately trying to make his autistic message understood. This is a creative act, an emotional cry of one human to another.

Don't be fooled by his ad-libs. Watch and listen carefully for the main theme, the main message.

The general and specific samples in this chapter will be of help, but they are by no means exhaustive. They cannot be, for each child is an individual. As a result, each child will create new sensoryisms, many of which are not mentioned here. These general rules and specific examples are given to you as a guide for looking, not as an exhaustive catalogue of isms.

The best place to start is alone in a room with the child. Be sure that it is reasonably quiet, that is, no air conditioning, traffic noise, general building noise, or conversations. Watch to see what in the room draws his attention. Sit very quietly but try to be as friendly as possible, without imposing yourself on the child. Don't move close to him; let him come toward you. Don't seem threatening by making any quick movements. Talk very quietly and naturally to him, but don't talk too much. When you have observed what intrigues him in the room, try to analyze his behavior. What sensory areas do his abnormalities encompass?

Now close your eyes and listen to him. You can learn a lot by listening to his movements, sounds, and the noises he creates with objects. Now move to another room and repeat the process. The different environment provides a new opportunity to make a completely new set of observations. Remember, *you* are often an intrusion to him, so, as you observe, become part of the room in every way possible.

Here are some general suggestions that will help you to observe and evaluate the behaviors.

One of the difficulties in observing the sensoryisms in children is our own sensory function, which often misleads us.

For instance, if we notice that every time a child comes into a room the family cat runs and hides, we might conclude that the cat ran away for self-protection. What happens to our conclusion when the child goes upstairs, bathes, and changes his clothes and the cat then comes to him and curls up in his lap?

A more tenable conclusion is that the child has played

with a neighbor's dog who routinely frightens the cat. The child arrives home to the cat smelling like the neighbor's dog. The cat runs away from that *smell*. We cannot smell the traces of telltale odor of the neighbor's dog as can the cat, and we draw an erroneous conclusion.

As another example I once asked an Oriental child, with whom I had established some rapport, about smell. I asked her to tell me if Caucasian people here in the United States smelled different in any way. She replied, "Oh, yes, you all smell like milk." Although we don't "smell like milk" to each other, because of our common diet, to her we have a distinctive odor.

I once knew a child who wouldn't watch television in his own home. He watched television avidly in his neighbor's house. One could conclude that he did not enjoy being in his own home. When I asked the child about not watching his own television, he told me he didn't "because it hurts." After much questioning and testing, I found that because the set needed repair, the home television set made a very high-pitched noise that none of us could hear. The noise was very painful to the child. With the television set repaired, the noise disappeared and the child became an avid home television viewer.

Be certain at all times that you attempt to look *beyond* your own normal sensory function as you watch the child and attempt to evaluate his behavior.

Remember that a child who moves *away* from you is probably *hyper* in one or more sensory systems.

Be especially sensitive to the child's behaviors as they relate to his head. Remember that the end organs (receptors) for vision, hearing, taste, and smell are all located in a very small area of the body, the face and head. Watch for which end organ he favors or rejects in his behavior.

Watch for any activity that diminishes the function of

an end organ of sensation. Covering the ears in any way, covering the nose, constantly trying to use dark glasses or covering the eyes are such indications. In general, diminishing the function of the end organ indicates a hyper system.

Many times you will have difficulty separating systems from each other in a behavior. For example, if a child moves away from you as you move toward him, it could be smell, tactility, or auditory. As a test, you can eliminate the auditory by being silent for a time before you approach the child. If he continues to move away, it could be tactility (the fear of you touching him) or it could be your smell. Remember, children who are hyper in smell can smell many more odors than normal and can detect faint odors that most of us cannot. Since we all have an odor about our bodies, many children with hyper smell are repulsed by us. To test for this, we can eliminate another sensation: tactility. Touch the child, run your hands over his arms and body. Is this the hypersensitive area?

With each observation write a list of the repetitive acts. Write down the activities from which he gains the greatest pleasure. Now you can categorize them into one of the following:

1. Tactility
2. Smell
3. Auditory
4. Taste
5. Vision

TACTILITY

Aristotle first pointed out the sense of tactility as the fifth sense. The other four senses had long been considered true senses because the end-organ of the sense to the outside world was obvious: Vision had eyes, hearing had ears, taste had the tongue, and smell had the nose. They were all specific and obvious.

But the skin was different. It covered the entire body and, as a result, was nonspecific. Before Aristotle the tactile sense was divided into many subsensations. He called them all tactility and listed *temperature, pain, pressure, and proprioception* as all part of the tactile sense. We feel temperature and pressure at, or near, the surface of the skin. We feel some deep pressure and pain. Proprioception is the sensing of body movement and changes in positions and relationships of various parts of the body through sensors within the joints and muscles. Proprioception is important in sensing balance. All four of these are part of tactility.

Tactility is the most ancient method of living organisms dealing with the world. The amoeba used it to survive, for when the amoeba touched something it enveloped it. Later came the pulsating creatures, such as sea slugs and snails, going to the highest form of squid and octopus. These creatures pulsate in order to increase the possibility of coming in touch with something tactile, hopefully food.

With segmentation the whole process blossomed into increasing motion, which increased the possibility for more tactile opportunity.

We all have lived through a period prior to birth when tactility was our supremely dominant sensation. During gestation we were surrounded by fluid, which gave us tactility in every way. It was our first sensory environment. It was the least demanding and most satisfying environment, since it gave us warmth, nutrition, safety, and some mobility, but tactility was its dominant sensory function.

As you observe for tactilisms be especially sensitive to

the child's reaction to temperature changes and to temperature extremes. Also watch for his reaction to pain and pressure—some rarely feel these and some will overreact to them. Watch for sensitivity to proprioception through watching his coordination of movements and his balance activities.

In evaluating tactilisms, look for any repetitive activity involving the skin. These will range from biting and hitting to stroking or gently tickling. Pay very special attention to the facial area and to the lips and nose. Conversely, look for any behavior which, in effect, blocks them in any way from the outside world.

Although the skin is considered the end organ for tactility, look for other areas of tactility, such as the tongue and mouth. Studies show that the sensitivity of the tip of the tongue to tactility and two-point discrimination is very great—perhaps the best in the body, including the highly sensitive fingers. The mouth is often used in tactility. The front of the mouth is much more tactilely sensitive than the back. The teeth, through pressure and some temperature sense, are also important in tactility.

The most important sensor of tactility is the hand. It is the tactile examiner that we use most often. It is highly mobile and the fingers are extremely sensitive. It is the key to such statements as "keep in touch." Observe the use of the hands very carefully.

Hypertactility

The key to hypertactility is the child's rejection of touch. He will resist being touched to the point of fighting. Human touch is the most noxious to him.

He is also repulsed by the touch of clothing (especially certain types of rough materials) or clothing that is restrictive. In general, he is repulsed by heat and cold variations. He does not enjoy water unless it is almost body temperature.

Quite often his body feels warm to the touch. His body also feels tense to the touch. He chooses soft or furry toys and will generally use the soft or furry toy to stroke his own body or to gently tickle his own body.

His tactilisms are usually very gentle if he is hypertactile. He will *gently* tickle or stroke himself in his efforts to normalize the tactile system.

Many hypertactile children appear as if they are masturbating. If they do touch their genitals, it is extremely gently. Quite often, they are so involved with the pleasurable gentle manipulation of some other part of the body that they do not become involved with the genital area in their tactilism.

Clothing problems, such as constant undressing, are difficult to categorize. Although they appear to be the result of hypertactilism, they can also be the result of hypersmell. Hypertactile children will resist clothing that is too rough or too restrictive—such as woolen or tweed trousers, or too-tight sweaters or collars. One has to doublecheck this, however, for quite often a child will resist clothing because of its smell. This is especially true of manmade fibers and those fabrics that have been treated for some forms of permanent press.

The hypertactile cannot tolerate great variations in temperature or pressure. They cannot tolerate pain and, in general, move away from tactility controlled by another person. They prefer tactility that they give themselves. This tactility is always gentle and always rhythmic.

Hypotactility

In extreme form, the hypotactile child can be seriously hurt and not cry. Such children often smile when spanked, ignore bruises or cuts, and seem generally unaware of their own body sensations. These are the *self-mutilating* children. They bite their bodies, stick pins into their skins, hit themselves, pinch fleshy portions of their bodies, or place their bodies in strangely contorted positions—all of which would be painful to us but which seem to give pleasure to the child who is hypotactile.

These children are most apt to carry out repetitive activity in which a large part of the body moves rhythmically, usually in a balancing activity. One must be careful in evaluating these gross body movements to be sure that one also evaluates the visual and auditory aspects.

Deep tactile activities of the hypotactile child are usually considered self-destructive by the observer. These are the children who bite their hands so you can hear their teeth grinding on the bones. These are the children who hurl their bodies through space at an object and have some black-and-blue areas or severely calloused areas, such as hands, arms, knees, elbows, or some part of the face.

They also pick at sores on their bodies so that, once they have a cut or bruise, they constantly pick at it, never allowing it to heal.

Tactility—White Noise

These children scratch nonexistent itches on their bodies. They often appear to be scratching nonexistent mosquito or fly bites.

Many times they will shiver as though some unseen object has touched them.

They seem to go along calmly for a period of time and suddenly display an outburst of tactile behavior, almost as though there were a gradual buildup of tactility coming from within their bodies.

These children are subject to "tactile outbursts" of hitting or slapping themselves or others. Following the outburst they are relatively quiet tactilely until another buildup occurs.

Look at their skins. Often the skin seems to "crawl." There is a rippling of the skin; the short hairs become erect for a few moments, then the skin and hair return to normal, for no apparent reason.

SMELL

Smell is the least understood area of behavior for autistic children. As a result, problems in this area are considered the most antisocial "isms," and these unfortunate young victims with problems of smell are the first to be rejected by our society.

Because we are a civilized and literate people, highly concerned with seeing and hearing, we tend to ignore the sense of smell. When problems arise in this area we frequently forget that smell was of primary importance at one time in our evolution and, as recently as our infancy, was the primary sensory channel.

Smell and taste are sometimes difficult to separate. Smell deals with chemicals in gaseous form, carried in the air. Taste deals with chemicals dissolved in liquid, carried in fluids.

The difficulty in discriminating between the two stems from their evolution. During the aquatic stage of life, the first smell organ had to detect smells that were water soluble. The Organ of Jacobson, located in the roof of the mouth of the aquatic creatures, served this purpose. Its function was to decide which particles of potential food borne in the water were to be directed back to the stomach and which particles were to be regurgitated; hence its placement in the roof of the mouth.

When animals came out into the air (amphibia and

primitive reptiles) they had to develop an additional smell system. The Organ of Jacobson was supplemented by a more human type of air-based smell organ in the nasal area. In these animals the two organs were very close to each other. As creatures evolved, the two systems became further divided. Both smell systems have been beautifully preserved in the python.

We humans have the vestigial (ancient and generally unused) Organ of Jacobson in the roof of our mouth, right behind the incisor teeth. This organ originally helped us to detect smell through water-soluble odors.

In addition, we have the olfactory membrane in the nose, through which we detect odors that are soluble in air. The olfactory membrane can be reached by air-laden odors through the nostrils and through the nasal air passages in the back of the throat. The two different systems are most separated in man, but they are still quite close together. Indeed, a thumb-sucking child may be dealing with tongue and lip tactility or with taste, but if he is stimulating the vestigial Organ of Jacobson, it also may be with *smell* that he is dealing.

Since, in general, our smells are the odors from the excretion of wastes from our bodies, what we put into our bodies (in terms of food) has a significant effect on what comes out as smell. Those of us who eat ample amounts of protein have a characteristic smell. To discover that smell, lick the top of your hand with your tongue, then smell your hand. This is your characteristic skin smell.

Remember that our bodies are geared for elimination of waste and that *waste smells*. We get rid of waste through our feces, our urine, our perspiration, and our breath. Many profitable industries are built around the aromatic functions of areas of our bodies, all of them aimed at changing or masking our smells. For hypersmellers such industries are failures, for these children are able to detect the smell despite all the attempts of products aimed at concealing our odors. Not only are millions of dollars spent annually in changing or masking our body smells, countless other millions are spent in changing or masking the odors outside our bodies. Clean air has become a byword, and we purify and filter as much air as we can to do away with odors.

We know a bit about one area: clothing smells. In our efforts to eradicate odors we wash or dry-clean our clothes. In addition, we add a masking aroma to the soap or cleansing agent to cover the remaining smell. We can do so only for a short period of time, for clothing absorbs our body odors quickly and it smells like we do.

In addition, much of our modern synthetic and permanent press-treated clothing retains its own (chemical) smell and our body odors as well, despite cleaning processes. As we spend more millions of dollars disposing of or improving our body smell (we have many antiodor agents for every body opening and for every waste disposal function), we are losing our battle against smells in our clothing and in the air about us.

As a result, the child with the problem of smell becomes more confused.

Hypersmell

The hyperolfactory child lives in a horrible world. As you know, dogs can smell our footsteps; they can trace our activities and they can follow or anticipate us at a great distance, often after a considerable amount of time has elapsed. Hyperolfactory children, with a doglike sense of smell, have many problems as a result of their too-acute ability to smell.

For them, although you have left the room, your essence remains. For them, you are surrounded by a complex and ever-changing signature of smell. Our smells change during each day and cyclically through each month. We, who have normal smell channels, are not cognizant of these changing signatures; indeed, we are often unaware that they exist.

We all have smells that we ignore, but these children cannot. They are repulsed by some, attracted by others, all of which significantly color their behavior.

Since smell is in the air and cannot be seen, these children have their attention stolen from us by an intangible stimulus. We, who have normal smelling abilities, not only can't see it, we can't smell it. This is why we misunderstand them so badly.

Remember that the hyperolfactory child can perceive smells at far greater distances than you can imagine. Some animals can detect a smell originating a mile away; normally man can only detect smells that originate much closer. Remember that this child can smell odors that you cannot detect, from sources much farther away than you realize, from other rooms and at times from other nearby homes.

Women must be especially conscious of their own body and breath odors during menstruation. A general rule of thumb to be followed with the hypersmell child is that "masking" (with deodorants, mouthwash, perfume, powder, sprays, etc.) does not hide the smells but, instead, merely adds more odors and renders your signature smell more confusing to the child.

Many of these children vomit when they smell their own urine. If they don't vomit, many are so nauseated by these smells that they refuse to urinate or defecate until they can no longer restrain themselves. They are so sensitive to smells that their *own wastes nauseate them.*

These children run from the waste of others, which is also nauseating to them. These are also the babies who fight at the breast. When a baby is first introduced to the breast, it is his ability to smell that guides him to the nipple. Children with hyperolfactory abilities cannot tolerate the pungent odor of the nipple and fight to get away from it. Hence, the phenomenon of fighting at the breast is a result of smell, not air starvation.

The change in the mother's metabolism as she nurses an infant frequently makes matters more difficult for the hypersmell children. Her body temperature rises and she begins to perspire as she nurses. This added smell makes it virtually impossible for the hyperolfactory child to tolerate being nursed at the breast. For the same reason, these same children later fight when being picked up or embraced. They can't tolerate the smell of the person picking them up.

Although we can't smell our own odors, these children can smell us, and the closer we are to them the more intense is our smell and their discomfort.

Watch your breath. It is a primary source of getting rid of smelly bodily wastes. Most of the tooth hygiene and mouthwashes help with solving and/or masking the smell problem, but they cannot change the fact that our breath smells because it contains wastes. We are unaware of these odors; the hypersmell child is *terribly aware* of these odors.

The hypersmell child is often a feeding problem. He cannot tolerate strong food odors and, when such odors increase, his rejective behavior increases. He does not eat food that has a strong odor, and he is often impossible to feed. He just can't bring himself close enough to food to taste it.

These children gag very easily. Strong odors or waste odors make them gag in situations where those of us with normal smell intake are oblivious to any smell being present.

Hyposmell

These are the children who are seeking intense smells. The most dramatic behavior indulged in is the smearing of their own feces on a wall or object, or on themselves. These children experience sheer joy when surrounded by strong, familiar smells.

Feces is our most potent waste material, in terms of smell. No other human waste product contains so much smell and so concentrated a smell. Differences in food intake change the character of our feces smell. To those of us with normal smell mechanism, feces smell is too concentrated and unpleasant. The hyposmell child finds feces the most potent, most pleasant, and most understandable waste smell.

These are the children who are apt to wet their beds or their night clothes, and these are the children who are apt to play with their own urine.

These are the children who go about smelling every object or person in a room before they do anything else. If you watch a dog smelling everything in his environment to see who urinated on it so as to place his unique signature (and sign of ownership) on each object, you can see what this child is doing. He is attempting to learn more about the object by moving closer to it and smelling it.

A child whose hands are constantly wet with saliva is usually a child with hyposmell. To understand this, smell such a child's hands and you will detect a pungent vinegar-like odor. The child uses the mixture of his own saliva and his skin to create the odor.

The child with hyposmell loves the strong smells of cooking. He tends to eat indiscriminately, quite often eating nonedible objects as food.

He tends to allow himself to accumulate wastes so that he has an odor. He is reassured by smelling his own odors, and the more intense, the better.

He enjoys being in the bathroom and is often reluctant to flush his own feces away.

He loves to smell people. He walks up to things and people, gets quite close and smells them. This child tries to read the smell signature of many objects by smelling anything he comes in contact with, and the stronger the smell the happier he is.

Smell—White Noise

These children have a constant smell in their olfactory systems. It is as though they have an inner odor that their noses can detect.

They will often place their hands over their mouth and nose and blow air from their mouth up to their nose in order to smell the odor of their breath (as we do to determine how desperately we need another dose of breath spray).

This child is apt to stuff small objects up into his nostrils in an attempt to change his smell mechanisms. Often he vacillates between going toward outside smells and running from them.

He occasionally breaks into very rapid breathing (hyperventilation), especially through his nose, almost in a seeming effort to clear out his nasal passages. He becomes quite tense whenever he has a cold or nasal congestion.

AUDITORY

A great many children with auditory isms are simply diagnosed as deaf. It is often difficult to differentiate the hypoauditory from the hyperauditory. This is the result of the hyperauditory child's attempts at self-preservation in our noisy world. He turns the auditory system off, so to speak, thus blocking *everything* out and appearing to be deaf. His face is usually an ashen gray color and he gives every indication of being deaf, in his attempt to survive in our sound-filled world, by turning off the sounds.

He allows sounds in only when he initiates them. If one observes such children for long periods of time, one notices that when quietly stimulating themselves, they tend to lose the ashen pallor. It tends to return when the outside world forces sound at them.

The organ of hearing is the ear. Problems might start with the outer portion of the ear. Gross displacement, such as large cupped ears, might gather more sound than flat, small ears. The openings to the inner ear are, on occasion, a factor; narrow passages, too-large passages, the presence or absence of wax, and the wax-collecting hairlike mechanisms in the ear can also influence hearing. The inner ear and balance are closely related. Hence, hearing and balance must be observed together. Bodily spinning or any "dizzying" activity that does not include the eyes usually involves hearing.

Children with problems of auditory (hearing) intake are usually the most difficult to manage *behaviorally*. Those children with hearing "isms" are generally rejected by the culture. This is because their behavior is often very difficult to understand and very difficult to control. 162871

Bathrooms are especially helpful in diagnosing auditory isms. Since the bathroom has many shiny, hard surfaces, sound bounces off them and reverberates through the bathroom quickly. There are few sound-deadening features, such as thick rugs and draperies; hence the sound is captured in the bathroom. In addition, there is the toilet, which makes noise when flushed. The tub and sink also produce noise.

The noises of water flow are bounced off the shiny, hard porcelain surfaces of the bathroom and its fixtures. If the walls are tiled, the sound reverberates more and longer. As a general rule those autistic children who love to play in the bathroom are probably hypoauditory, and those who resist going into the bathroom are probably hyperauditory.

In evaluating for auditory isms, any activity that produces a sound is to be sought. Periodically close your eyes and listen to the child. These sounds will range from vocal sounds to lip smacking, ear tapping, and hitting objects together incessantly. Listen for the rhythm of all the noises the child makes. Can you *hear* a rhythm? Watch for rhythmic balancing that doesn't seem to include the use of his eyes. These balancing acts would usually make one dizzy if his eyes were open, but do not cause these kinds of children to become dizzy.

Do *not* use music to evaluate the hearing function. Music changes the listening set of children with auditory problems. Such children often learn about objects by palpating them. They tap the object with a finger and listen for differences in sounds, as they tap different parts of the object, much as the physician does as he taps your chest and listens to the sounds with his stethoscope. When palpating won't work, these children will tear or break an object, carefully studying the sounds it makes as it is destroyed.

Hyperauditory

It is important to understand that the hyperauditory child can tolerate his own noise quite well so, when evaluating auditory performance for hyper- or hypo-, the noise must come from outside the child.

Hyperauditory performance is usually one of avoidance or rejection. The child will move away from a noise or sound. If he cannot get far enough away, he will close off his ears by using his hands over them, putting his fingers inside them, or by completely rejecting the sound. In the latter situation he will test as, or appear to be, totally deaf. He is hurt by sounds and, since he can't stop them through moving away or through stopping up his ears, *he turns them off in his brain.* Such a child does not even jump when a loud noise goes off behind him.

His face is usually ashen gray in color and his behavior gives the impression that he is totally deaf. This transitory deafness disappears as soon as he begins to make a repetitive noise of his own. He listens to his own noises with pleasure.

Occasionally the *hyper*auditory child will move *toward* sound. These sounds are usually soft and coming from people. They are usually whispers. When whispering, do not get so close that your breath can be felt at the outer ear, for often this will force the child back into sound rejection.

Remember that the hyperauditory child hears many sounds that we, with normal hearing, do not hear.

He has problems sleeping through noise that we ignore; often he hears sounds that we do not know exist or that we are able to exclude from our consciousness. He is a very light sleeper, often not sleeping through the night.

Many electrical and mechanical devices make high-pitched noises that we cannot hear, but that hyperauditory children do hear. This can be seen in those children who listen to and hear seemingly nonexistent noises from light bulbs, water pipes, drying clothes, breathing, television sets, and so on.

The hyperauditory child is frightened by animals. Their sounds frighten him, first because animals make sounds at unpredictable times, such as a cat purring or a dog barking. In addition, many of the sounds are too loud to be handled comfortably.

Haircuts are a special terror to the hyperauditory child. Not only does the snipping of scissors frighten him beyond control, the electric hair trimmer, with its noise near his ear, is terrifying.

Indeed, anything going near his ears, even if not noisy, is terrifying. Cleaning and washing his ears is excruciating torture for him.

Heavy breathing, snoring, and wind-caused house noises are all terror-producing for the hyperauditory child.

He is frightened by crowds, tunnels, traffic, and sirens. These sounds happen unexpectedly and are too loud to be handled comfortably. Their very loudness makes them *painful* to the child.

Wind presents a problem for the hyperauditory child. It is a sound that is unpredictable because its source can't be seen and it is variable. The high-pitched noises coming from nowhere are often frightening, and their constantly changing characteristics are also a problem to the hyperauditory child. This loud and variable sound, coupled with very little evidence of its creation (it comes from nowhere) can be disturbing to the hyperauditory child.

The most basic result of a snowstorm is that it muffles the sound environment. Consequently, the hyperauditory child has to adjust to a completely new world of sound. Often he will sit as though in a trance, either listening to the quiet or waiting for it to stop.

Rainstorms are especially difficult for the hyperauditory child. Not only does the thunder send him into paroxysms of fright, but the rain patter on the roof is exaggerated for him and, as a result, sounds like muffled thunder.

Hyperauditory children, when they cannot control the pain and fright of the noise in their environment, often attempt to leave the source of the noise. This avoidance re-action can take the form of leaving the room, hiding in a closet, or hiding under the bed covers, all the way to running away from home.

Hiding under a cover can be either hypervisual or hyperauditory. Watch to see what precipitates this reaction—sound or sight.

Paging through books makes a quiet, soothing sound. This can be confused with visualisms, and thus must be observed carefully.

The hyperauditory child does not like any constant sound in his environment, such as a noisy air-conditioning or heating system. He especially dislikes the sound of the surf at the seashore.

These are the "runaway" children you read about periodically. When the sound is too loud to handle, or is too variable to handle, the child tries to stop it by covering his ears, covering his body, or by moving away from the sound. When all this fails, he runs away. Newspapers often carry stories of the "special" child who wanders away from his family or school group. The entire community turns out for the search. Generally, the search is too noisy. The child has run away from the sound he couldn't handle. He hides in a quiet place seeking peace. Noise will further frighten him. A quiet search must be carried out.

Hypoauditory

This is the banger, the shouter, the child for whom the world is too quiet. Not enough of the sound message of the world reaches his brain; hence he seeks more sound in greater frequency and in greater intensity.

He makes loud, rhythmic noises and moves *toward* them. He places his ear up against vibrating and noisy surfaces. He loves noises and loud sounds. He moves toward them and often sits for hours listening to a washing machine, or dishwasher, electric mixer, or vacuum cleaner. He enjoys being in the kitchen and/or bathroom, the two noisiest rooms in the house (especially if tiled and uncarpeted). He constantly flushes the toilet, runs the water, or moves closer to electric appliances that are noisy.

A good deal of sonar-type sound bouncing is observed. The child will move around an object or a wall, making sounds and listening to how the sound echo differs with each position.

He adores the seashore and will sit listening to the sound of the surf. Garbage trucks are especially fascinating to him, as are fire engines and ambulances. He loves to listen to loud lawn mowers and loud engines of any type, especially if the engines make a rhythmic noise.

He loves to tear paper—stiff paper, not "quiet" paper, such as facial tissues. He enjoys the noise that the tearing paper makes as he rips it. Also, he enjoys crumpling paper in his hands or ripping sheets of paper off a tablet.

Doors are a special problem and a special delight for the hypoauditory child. He loves to close and open them with varying force. There are times when he will slam doors with reverberating force. He seems destructive in his search for sound, almost as if he were breaking things apart to see what sound is contained within.

In evaluating toys, look especially for spinning and moving parts and listen for noise. If the toy is silent, the problem is usually visual. If it is noisy, it is probably auditory. Listen to the toys carefully. Do they rub or squeak? Hypoauditory children enjoy squeaky and belltype toys.

The hypoauditory loves crowds, such as at the circus, and he likes traffic noises. Often he will sit staring vacantly, allowing the sounds of the environment into his auditory system.

These children love sounds of all types.

Auditory White Noise

These children seem preoccupied with their own internal sounds. After they have run, they might sit quietly listening to their own heartbeats. Following a meal, they might sit and listen to their own digestive systems at work.

These children will often hyperventilate (breathe rapidly) through their mouths and listen to their own breathing. They then often vary their breathing rate, listening to themselves in rapture.

These children often have violent screaming outbursts, for no apparent reason.

These are the children who often rock (especially their heads) and then stop almost as if listening to the difference in noises in their heads.

They assume strange gravitational positions, such as hanging over a chair, head down or head on an angle. They seem to be listening to themselves.

They are often hummers. They make a constant quiet noise and listen to it.

TASTE

The primary organ of taste is the tongue. The tongue contains roughly ten thousand tiny taste buds. Their work in aggregate is to make four basic decisions about taste: sour, salty, bitter or sweet, which are our only tastes.

The tip of the tongue is most sensitive to salt and sweet tastes. The sides of the tongue are sensitive to sour, and the back of the tongue is sensitive to bitter tastes.

Anything that has a taste, when placed in the mouth, is evaluated by the tongue according to these four tastes. If the object is chewed and odors escape, they float up into

the nasal cavity. When they come in contact with the olfactory membrane we experience smell.

As a rough rule of thumb, children who are hyper in
taste tend to use the tip of their tongue for tasting. They
are monitoring sweet and salty foods and objects. Those
who are hypo in taste tend to use the sides and back of
their tongues; they are monitoring sour and bitter. Those
with white noise in their taste systems tend to stimulate
and suck on the sides and backs of their tongues, monitoring mostly sour and bitter tastes.

The tongue also is extremely sensitive tactilely. It is
sometimes difficult to separate the taste and tactile functions of the tongue. Food habits are helpful in making this
separation. Food preferences, based on consistency, indicate tactility. Food decisions, based on taste, indicate taste.

Since only in taste and tactility does the child have to
come into contact with the object to be sensed, it is sometimes difficult to separate the two functions. Because man
has such sophisticated audition and vision, through spoken
and written language, his former dependence on taste and
smell have become more limited.

Children will often taste a whole category of things, such
as everything in a room that is of one color. They will often
run their tongues over separate objects and will also lick
people to learn more about them. These children often give
clear indications of their problems through tasting things.
Watch a child eat a cigarette. If he spits it out, he is hyper.
If not, he is hypo.

A high percentage of those with tasteisms do not enjoy
eating sweets. The children with hypertaste gag easily at
strong tastes and move away from them. They are usually
extremely poor eaters and, if they do eat, will eat only
bland foods. The hypotasters eat anything. They have no

food discriminations and often eat nonedible or even horrible-tasting foods.

Hypertaste

Children who are hyper in taste very early in life push away food that is too stimulating to their taste channel. They become extremely picky eaters. Some of them barely survive their hypertaste.

I saw one twelve-year-old child who had never eaten anything except Pablum and milk! I saw a six-year-old girl who, once weaned from a bottle, never ate anything but raw apples! Other foods were just too taste stimulating for these children and were rejected by them.

These children are the early feeding problems, for their tolerance of variations in taste is extremely limited. They detest bubbly drinks and will throw them, if surprised by the bubbles.

Hypotaste

We can call these children the garbage pails of our group, for they will eat anything and everything. These children are dangerous to themselves, in that they will eat or drink materials that are extremely poor in taste, such as gasoline, and various poisonous materials that they might discover, such as paint. These are the children whose stomachs are pumped out routinely because of their lack of discrimination as to what they eat or drink. They put *everything in their mouths*.

Taste—White Noise

These children have a constant *taste* in their mouths. If one watches such a child he acts as though he is sucking his own tongue and cheeks in order to gain a taste from them. When this doesn't satisfy, these children often regurgitate their recently consumed food and rechew it, retaste it, and then reswallow it.

Their taste experience seems to come from within. These children are usually apathetic about food. They will allow someone to feed them, but rarely do they feed themselves.

They will often have thick tongues. This is the result of their tasting their own saliva. They do this by sucking their own tongues, with the focus of the sucking at the sides. With enough sucking, the tongue becomes both wider and thicker.

VISION

In many ways, vision is man's proudest achievement. Man has refined the use of his visual system to the point that most researchers consider vision to be our most used sensory channel. It is the sense that has the greatest distance variation. We can see objects a few inches away from our eyes, and we can see stars in space.

Next to the skin, the eyes are the most exposed sensory organs. We can watch them function. We're never quite sure of what goes on inside the ear, inside the nose, or inside the mouth, but the eyes give many outward indications of how they are being used.

To evaluate for visual isms, look for anything that contains a body movement, such as rocking, spinning, or twirling. Watch for any movement that takes place in front of the eyes. Also, look for any compulsive watching of moving objects, such as automobiles, open clocks, or records spinning on a record player.

Look also for any objects that are extensions of the blind man's cane, such as sticks, ropes, or long toys that are carried out in front of the child or are spun in the air, as visual indicators.

Most rhythmic movements of objects within the visual field, but which don't make noise, are visual indicators. Bodily spinning, rocking, and erratic or quick movements are often visual indicators.

If the child is hypervisual, too much sensation arrives at the brain; hence a small speck of dust might capture this child's visual attention. If he is hypovisual, not enough sensation gets into the brain, so there is much rhythmic body movement, especially in relation to light sources. Visual white noise occurs when the eyes themselves are touched or hit rhythmically. You can create your own white noise by closing your eyes and pushing on your lids with your fingers. You will have the illusion of seeing various forms of light and, if you press or hit your closed eyes, you can make yourself see all kinds of displays, all the way up to seeing stars.

Hypervision

This child constantly looks at minute particles of dust or minute articles in his environment. He might spend hours picking lint off a rug or off his clothes. He might find a small piece of dust and stare at it for hours.

Sudden, but controlled, movements are a trademark of the hypervisual child. These movements can be from side to side, allowing the child to see, as though he were moving his eyes from right to left; or back and forth, allowing the child to move to and from an object. These movements are always carefully controlled.

These children love wheels, clocks with visibly turning parts, records spinning, and tops, all of which, if watched too long and too intently, form optical illusions. These children are rarely, if ever, fooled by optical illusions.

These are the children who are often mistakenly called idiots savants because of their fantastic visual memory. They can recall almost everything they see, and we are astounded by their visual recall. They often read phenomenally well. Also, they frequently read strange materials, such as Shakespearean plays, the telephone book, or automobile licenses with almost total recall.

Children who are hyper in vision often spend hours staring at a saliva drop between their fingers. They use the drop of saliva (or water, or a glass) as both a magnifier of light and a distributor of light into varying colors. These children love to look through pinholes, through distorted glass, and are fascinated by small, intricate objects. They will take a single strand of hair and pull it taut and then stare up and down the hair, often using it as a sighting hair for more distant objects.

Usually these children dislike mirrors and do not enjoy seeing themselves, either in a mirror, in a water reflection, or in photographs.

The creation of extremely intricate designs is one of their favorite pastimes. Such children will often draw designs or move objects to create designs and patterns that they find fascinating.

The moon and stars fascinate these children. So do airplanes, clouds, and high bridges. These are stared at carefully and for long periods of time.

Usually, these children are afraid of the dark. They are frightened by sharp flashes of light, lightning, and they do not like bright sunshine. This sort of child would be miserable if his family spent the summer vacation at a beachfront house on the seashore.

Hypovision

Rocking is a keynote for the hypovisual child. He either rocks back and forth, moving the object viewed from near to far, or from side to side, or moving the object viewed from side to side.

The second keynote is his great attraction to light sources, going from the sun (which can be dangerous to his eyes) to pinpoints of light. This child spends very much time staring at the sun streaming through windows. Not only does he stare at the sun, but also he is intrigued by the shadow lines in the sun. The sharper the shadows, the more he is intrigued.

A behavior difficult to understand is a slow walking around an object, staring intently while circling. This is really an attempt to line up the edge of the object, to understand its position in space.

Often, a hand (tactility) is run around the edge of the object (such as a table or chair) as the child studies the object. He may also choose to push a wheeled toy along the edge of the object for hours on end. He is fascinated by edges of objects and may spend hours rolling a toy up to the edge, trying to gauge the edge without having the toy fall.

The hypovisual child is afraid of heights, stairs, and dark tunnels, and he is often fearful of speed. His visual abilities cannot cope with speed and with depth.

Turning of objects, such as pencils, must be observed closely. If done in front of the eyes, it is visual. This is one of the most common forms of visualism and can encompass innumerable objects.

Often the child will step back and forth from one colored surface to another, such as where two differently colored rugs meet. He may step back and forth for hours on end in his attempt to normalize his visual system. I have often seen such children fall when they came to a place where two differently colored rugs abutted each other. In essence, they fell down because of the change in color.

These children are especially intrigued with mirrors or other shiny-surfaced objects—for example, shiny pots, dishes, glass, or doorknobs. They will stare at them for hours, rhythmically moving the shiny surface, or their own bodies, and watching the changing reflections.

Another thing these children love to do is bend coat hangers or wire. Then they look at the new shape. They bend the metal again and stare at it, almost as if attempting to stop a changing object long enough to study it before they change it again. They change it by bending it, then look at it almost as if to see if what they saw were correct.

Finger twisting and hand play are fairly universal among the hypovisual children. These activities are always carried out within the field of vision.

Rubber bands are also used. They are stretched and used as sighting markers, or are stared at as they stretch and go through the air.

Wind blowing leaves, or wind blowing objects into a swaying motion, is always intriguing. Often, such children will blow an object themselves and watch it move. This is most often done with small pieces of paper or dust.

These children are also throwers. They throw relatively light objects and watch them. They rarely throw heavy objects, as do the hypoauditory children.

Vision—White Noise

This child very often has dilated pupils. He not only looks through people, he also looks, often, through things. He acts as though he is watching something very carefully, but something that is situated *within* his eyeball. He sees as though his eyes weren't turned out to the world, but turned in toward himself. He looks as though he is seeing things that aren't there.

This child often touches, pulls at, rubs, or hits his eyes

to make internal flashes of light appear in his visual system. He is obsessed with the eyes, and much of his repetitive action includes his eyes.

Although none of the visualism children make eye contact (looking you in the eye) readily, this child finds it impossible even when forced to do so. His is a distorted visual experience, and whatever sensation he allows in adds to the distraction. He acts the most like a truly blind person. His attention is constantly upon a world that isn't there. Most of what he sees is distorted and is an illusion, and comes from within.

Now that you have watched your child, you must come to a decision: Which channel or channels are affected? How? Hyper, hypo, or white noise? Wait a few days and repeat your observation and evaluation. Remember, these general rules and specific examples are given as a guide for your observation, not as an exhaustive catalogue of isms. They cannot be, for each child is an individual; he creates his own isms, some of which may not be mentioned here.

If your child exhibits isms in more than one sensory channel, make a list of the channels affected and the isms under each. This will help you to decide with which channel you should start to work. Always start with the channel in which the child exhibits the greatest number of isms.

When you have made enough observations to decide which sensory channel or channels are affected and how, you are ready to move on to treatment for survival.

IX
TREATING FOR SURVIVAL

TREATMENT

Treatment, if it is to have a chance for success, must proceed in two stages:

Stage 1: The Survival Stage
The goal of this stage is to eliminate the sensoryisms. This enables the child's behavior to become more acceptable to those around him. Freeing him of the sensoryisms that have *monopolized* his attention allows him to begin to pay attention to the sensations to which we *want* him to pay attention. Freeing the child from the sensoryisms also enables him to pay attention to the activities of the next stage.

Stage 2: Central Treatment
The goal of this stage is to change the child's development enough so that he can be integrated into society insofar as possible—both behaviorally and educationally.

The Survival Stage
Most children who fail do so at the survival stage. Survival versus abandonment is a frightening choice. It is diffi-

cult to imagine the pain, the fear, the hopelessness that leads a parent to consider abandonment. This is a difficult subject to discuss, especially with parents who are on the brink of abandonment.

I had many discussions with tearful mothers who were on the verge of casting their lot for abandonment. We discussed the chronology of despair that led them to this point. Surprisingly, *it was not the behavior that was intolerable, it was not the behavior that was the primary cause for their considering abandonment.* What brought them to the brink of abandonment was that they could not understand *why* the child behaved as he did. These were their reactions:

"It's not so much what he does that's deranged, but there's no reason for his doing what he does. That's what the problem is."

"His behavior is odd, but tolerable. To want to behave that way for no cause, no reason, is what makes me think he's psychotic."

"I could take the strange behavior—if only it had some purpose."

"If there were some reason for his strange behavior that I could understand, then I could even accept the behavior."

I watched these mothers as I explained my theory to them. Tears vanished and attitudes changed. Now they had at least a theoretical reason "why" for their child's strange behavior. Now the behavior didn't seem so strange. I found that the child's opportunity for survival was dramatically increased when the parents *understood* a possible cause for the behavior. *Even though the same behavior continued,* it could now be tolerated, because it was no longer considered meaningless or deranged by the parent. *It now seemed to be meaningful behavior, and, therefore, understandable and acceptable.*

I found that when the parents were involved in the evaluation of the behavior, when the parents understood the theory, a big step toward survival was taken. Indeed, parental *understanding* of the child's behavior became the biggest single step toward the child's survival.

As a result, *parental understanding of the behavior became the first goal of the survival stage.*

The second goal of the survival stage is to help the child to *rid himself of his sensoryisms so that he will not be rejected* or declared hopeless by those around him. In this stage we must deal directly with the child's sensory problems in order to effect an immediate change in his behavior.

The third goal of the survival stage is to *free the child of his strange sensory addiction, which monopolizes his attention.* Once freed from this monopoly, he can begin to allow the real world into his nervous system. Once freed, he can move on to the next stage of treatment.

In order to succeed at survival, we must:

1. Understand the behavior. If the *reason for* behavior is understood, it is much easier to tolerate. What we *understand* is much less disturbing to us. *Understanding leads to acceptance.*
2. Alter the environment in order to decrease the child's sensory discomfort.
3. Alter the environment in an attempt to decrease sensoryisms.
4. Insofar as possible, we can alter the function of the sensory end-organ from which the sensoryisms are initiated.
5. Through treatment we can help the child to begin to normalize the sensory channel or channels that are not normal.

The following are suggestions for increasing the possibility of survival. They are by no means all-inclusive, but are techniques that we have found useful. Since each child is different, other techniques may be needed. Use these as a guide, modifying them as needed.

TACTILITY

Be cognizant of the four dimensions of tactility. Remember, they are: *temperature, pain, pressure,* and *proprioception*—the feeling of movement.

Remember that, although the skin is the over-all end-organ of tactility, the mouth, tongue, and teeth are sensitive tactilely.

The hand is the most specific and most active tactile portion of our bodies. It is the tactile hunter or searcher, which is used most when the body is quiet. The whole body is tactilely sensitive. To be tactilely perceived, the object or person must come in contact with the child's body, except in the area of temperature.

Hypertactility

Remember that this child is very disturbed by tactility that he does not control or initiate. Tactility monopolizes his thoughts and is the source of his fears.

Clothing which is rough, scratchy, tight, or heavy should be eliminated. He will be frightened by pressure on his body, so any body contact, such as hugging, should be gentle. He will be extremely frightened by pain and, as a result, will be apprehensive of doctors and dentists. A small pain, such as having an eyelash in his eye, can make him hysterical. Protect him from painful tactility insofar as possible.

You may have great difficulty bathing him, and he will scream when you cut his toenails or fingernails. Remember, to him, this hurts. Be careful also of rough towels.

He will have a tendency to feel warm to the touch and to perspire easily. Keep the temperature of the house on the low side and be sure that, when indoors, he removes sweaters. He is also hypersensitive to cold, so try to maintain the temperature as evenly as possible.

Permit him to play with body positions such as twisting his fingers and sitting in odd positions, at the outset of treatment. These are proprioceptive feelings that reassure him. As he makes progress, begin to replace these with activities more appropriate to his age, and with more varied proprioceptive activities.

Remember that he is exceedingly *ticklish*. Even a small breeze can dramatically change his behavior. Keep to a minimum any unpleasant tactility with which he has to cope. Ask people not to touch or handle him. Don't smother him with tactility. Remember, it can be unpleasant to him.

Watch him as he carries out his own tactilisms. Find one that gives him great pleasure. *Try to do to him what he is doing to himself.* For example, if he is stroking his cheek, you begin to stroke his cheek, gently. When he tolerates this, go to another tactilism he enjoys. Try to do *to* him tactilely what *he* is doing to himself. As he tolerates your doing it, he will begin to tolerate variations. For example, now you no longer need to stroke only his cheek, you can move on to stroking his head, or neck, and so forth. The first goal is to build in the child a tolerance for tactile stimulation—coming from outside himself and controlled by someone other than himself.

Next, start to gently stimulate his face with a very light touch with your fingers. Go over his entire face back to his ears with a gentle stroking action. He may grimace or resist at the outset. As he begins to accept this gentle stroking, name each part of the face as you touch it.

Next, start stimulating his rib cage, arms, and hands. Do this stroking with the palm of the hands at the outset. As he begins to tolerate it, return to very light stroking, using your fingertips. Always tell him what you are touching. If it becomes too unbearable to him, stop for a while, then start again.

Hypotactility

This child *needs as much tactile stimulation as possible*. He needs variations in temperatures in his daily surroundings. He requires proprioceptive experience. Move his arms and legs, and run with him. He will enjoy pressure, very much enjoy aggressive bear hugs, and will like fairly strenuous tickling. If he uses body rhythms, try to capture them by joining in, expanding and exaggerating them.

His skin needs much attention. Be sure to brush his skin, tickle it, rub it with a coarse, rough towel. Vary the temperature of his bath water while he is in the tub. Massage him deeply; also pinch his skin. Help the message to get through to the brain from the skin by *increasing the frequency* with which you do these activities, by *increasing the intensity* with which you stimulate his skin, and by *increasing the duration* with which you apply the stimuli. Above all, *increase the variety* of tactile inputs as much as you can.

Be especially cognizant of areas of the body that he hits, hurts, mutilates, picks at, or are calloused from overuse. These are the areas that need more stimulation. Remember that he has a diminished sensitivity to pain. Be certain to protect him from stimulation that will do him harm.

Use vibrations from appliances or even a small vibrator

to give him tactile stimulation. Many such children enjoy a vibratory massage over the entire body.

When he becomes able to accept some tactility coming from the outside, you can begin a more consistent approach. Begin with his most used tactile activity. This is usually the hand and forearm, although not exclusively so.

Give the hand and arm great variations in temperature. This can be done through immersing them into alternately heated and then cold water. Be careful of the heated water. Even though he does not *feel* pain, he is easily burned. Put your own hand in first. Rub and massage the outside of both the hand and forearm slowly and vigorously. Pinch them and slap them, constantly being careful not to hurt them. Be sure that you also give them deep pressure through kneading. Now move the arm and hand about. Also move the fingers. Apply some resistance to his movement, especially to his finger movement. When finished, rub the hand and forearm with a rough towel.

Tactility—White Noise

Never use a vibrator with this child and *do not* allow him to tactilely enjoy the vibration of the household appliances.

This child needs to experience much tactile stimulation coming from *outside* himself. His first goal is to learn the difference between internally caused tactility and externally initiated tactility. Each time he is given a tactile stimulus there must be a definite, obvious indication of its source.

For example, if he is to be tickled, be obvious about the fact that you are going to tickle him. This is not the place for subtlety. Show him your finger, exaggerate your tickling motion, and tell him you are going to tickle him, before you actually do. Then, tell him you *are* tickling him while the tickling is in progress.

The next step is to help him to differentiate between different types of tactility coming from outside his own body and controlled by some person other than himself.

He must be shown each tactile input and have it explained beforehand *and* during the stimulation. At this stage he needs to be able to contrast and to compare two different tactile inputs. For example, "I'm going to squeeze you, then I'm going to lift you up." While you do each of these actions, tell him again what you are doing. Then take two other tactile activities and follow the same routine.

As he begins to tolerate and understand *outside versus his inside* tactility, you can begin to give him a great variety of tactile experiences. You must constantly be at him tactilely. The less time he has for being involved with his own inner tactility the more time he will have to spend with outside tactility. In essence, he needs outside tactility experience as constantly as possible—of temperature, pain, pressure, and proprioception. Be sure to name each tactile experience and be sure that you tell him what it will be, *before* you do it.

As his tolerance grows, change the rhythm. You must not only dictate the tactility, you must also dictate the *rhythm*. Always make your tactile rhythm different; constantly vary it. Repetition is very important and very helpful in teaching this child.

SMELL

This is the least understood area of behavior for autistic children. The primary problem is not the child, it is the rest of the world. Because of this, those of us with normal smell capacities have great difficulty understanding the problems involved with smell.

You must try to gain new insights into your own ability to smell if you are to help these children to survive. Remember that body wastes have a particular and strong smell, and that living organisms must constantly produce waste if they are to live.

Because smell is *not* one of civilized man's primary sensory channels, we must be sure to be overly sensitive and aware in dealing with children who have smellisms. We must try hard to understand the problem. Much observation in this area often is a helpful means of acquiring insight and understanding.

Hypersmell

We need to understand that each of our bodies is surrounded by a series of smells and that our smells change. We need to move closer to these children very slowly, always remembering that our bodies give off a strong odor. Covering up body smells with other smells rarely works with these children. It just tends to confuse them. Fresh air is a good antidote for smell.

Bathrooms and kitchens should be very well ventilated at all times. Strong odors, no matter how pleasant they might seem, are to be discouraged. This includes air sprays, deodorants, tooth paste, after-shave lotion, hair spray, cologne, and perfume.

Clothes should be cleaned with nonsmelly solutions and laundered with nonsmelly soaps or detergents. Washing a child's face with a washcloth that has been hanging, damp, for a few hours can be a horrifying experience, because the cloth develops a smell that is unpleasant for these hypersmell youngsters. Diapers are especially noxious and should be placed out of the smell area of the child.

Household odors should be kept to a minimum, especially strong cooking odors and food odors. Cabbage, Brussels sprouts, and fish odors might cause nausea. Food for these children should be bland and nonaromatic.

As the child's smell environment becomes less smell threatening, start giving him gentle and mild smells. Tell him what the smell will be, what the smell is, and then bring the smell close to him and repeat, once again, what the smell is. *Don't put it under his nose!* He can smell from greater distances than you can imagine. It is better to have the smell too far away than too close.

Tell him what it is, even though he doesn't seem to be paying any attention. Be sure that there are no other smells in the air to confuse him.

Spend much time outdoors in a nonsmell-polluted environment.

Explain to those around him that their smells affect him. Menstruating women should increase their distance from him.

When he is at the point where he can tolerate mild, gentle, and somewhat distant smells, begin to introduce *people* smells, remembering that they are the most waste-laden.

Bring people closer to him, let him smell them, have them sit closer to him. Cover his eyes as he progresses, and ask him, "Who is this?" "What is this?" If he doesn't know, tell him and let him smell again.

Remember, you are teaching him to live with, to tolerate smells that he cannot control. As he improves, vary the smells and include more household smells, moving him as close to a normal smell environment as possible.

Hyposmell

This child needs great intensity of smells in his environment. House odors, clothing odors, and waste odors should be given to the child at every turn. Have him smell his soiled diaper, if an infant. Have him smell his own feces; have him smell aromatic foods, but with each smell *tell him what it is!* Don't comment on its pleasantness or unpleasantness to you; just name the smell for him.

Give him pungent smells in as pure form as possible. When presenting the smells, be sure that they are not contaminated by other smells. Place the items to be smelled right under the child's nose. Always tell him what the smell is. As he progresses, give him less intense smells and move them farther away from his nose.

He is now ready to learn to discriminate between different smells. Start with two fairly strong but very different smells. Play a game with him. Can he recognize which smell is *vinegar,* with his eyes closed? As he progresses in discrimination, move the smells farther away and use milder smells for the game.

You can now begin to discourage his interest in the smelling of wastes. Be sure that all toilets are flushed immediately and begin to store diapers and soiled clothing in air-tight containers. You can also, at this time, begin to discourage his up-close smelling of objects and people. The goal is to increase the distance from which he smells objects. If he has to put his nose on them to smell them, for all practical purposes they have no smell. He must learn that smell is carried through the air and it comes to him. He must wait for it, he must not go to it.

Smell—White Noise

The goal is to have this child begin to react to smells that come from *outside* his own body. Use a household deodorant so that the house is relatively smell-free. Use smell-free clothing cleaners and laundry products. The goal is to create a relatively smell-free environment, so be sure that the child is also smell-free.

Each day put on the child and his clothing *a separate* unique smell. Put a drop or two on his body and on the fabric of his clothes. You can use after-shave lotion, vinegar, a specific cologne or perfume, kerosene, ammonia, etc. These smells must be specific and easily differentiated from other smells. Most perfumes smell too much like each other to be unique enough to be useful. The smells must be varied—daily. They become the child's "smell for the day"!

Each morning tell him what his "smell for the day" will be. As he progresses, choose smells that are not so highly specific and reduce their intensity.

After a few weeks of the "smell for the day" approach, begin to introduce other smells. He will have to learn to differentiate between his "smell for the day" and the smell you now give him. Be sure to show it to him, describe it, then have him smell it. As he begins to react to these *outside* smells, gradually cut down the strength of the "smell for the day." When he reacts well to the presented smells, stop the "smell for the day" and continue to develop his smell discrimination by presenting smells and having him recognize them with his eyes closed.

Repetition is very important and very helpful in teaching this child.

AUDITORY

Children with auditory problems are captives of their environment. The environment is extremely important as it relates to sound. Some environments absorb sound, others reflect it. The environment can be changed easily, and the auditory behavior will change as a result.

The source of sound, other than the sound created by the child himself, is also a problem. These youngsters need to learn where the sound originates and who controls the sound or creates it.

Children with auditory problems generally adore music, unless it becomes too loud. The transition from making his own sound to listening to sound controlled by someone else is the most important goal.

Hyperauditory

The greatest problem with this child is that he *turns off* all sounds coming from some source other than himself. He listens only to the sounds *he* makes and controls. Often he acts totally deaf to the sound made by others. Frequently he goes through life considered deaf and is "tested" deaf.

He should be surrounded by a sound-absorbing environment, e.g., rugs, draperies, acoustical tile ceilings—not bare floors, tile walls, shutters or blinds in lieu of curtains.

Keep him away from social gatherings, crowds, the beach, anything that externally forces sounds on him.

Don't force him into bathrooms or kitchens that are untreated for sound absorption. They will be too noisy for him.

Don't frighten him with loud noises or unpredictable noises. Noises coming from nowhere are especially frightening. Always warn him of thunderstorms or sirens. Never shout at him!

Keep him away from noisy animals and noisy places, such as airports, concerts, parties, ball games, or noisy traffic.

Balance is often a problem, due to his overly sensitive inner ears. He will be prone to carsickness and vertigo, if spun or moved too rapidly.

Be careful about where he sleeps. Be sure that it is a quiet part of the house. Be sure that there are no house creaks, furnace noises, animal fights, trains, traffic noises, or airline routes overhead. All of these disturbances will interfere with his sleep. If there is no way to provide him with a quiet environment for sleep, turn on a radio that plays uninterrupted and quiet music to serve as background music while he sleeps. This musical background will tend to "mask" the noises that ordinarily wake him up. He will be able to sleep, undisturbed by noises that are alarming to him.

Be sure always to prewarn him of any noises or of any over-all changes in his sound environment. This is especially true when going on trips, having visitors, or moving.

These children can become "runaway" children. Be careful in supervising such a child, particularly in new environments that might include crowds, many guests, or involve any significant change in the noise level of his "sound" environment. When searching for a "runaway," be certain to conduct a quiet search. Remember, he usually runs away from the sound and will seek a quiet place to hide, frequently underneath something like a canvas or a blanket, and farthest from the source of the sound that is offensive to his sensitive ears.

If the sound environment is too difficult for him to handle, and if you cannot change it, buy a pair of swimmer's earplugs. Put them into his ears. This will cut down the incoming sound and will raise his tolerance for the noisy situation. There are also sterile waxes that one can purchase. They are fitted into the ears and serve the same purpose of eliminating noise for him. This should be done only for survival, not treatment.

This child requires a lot of quiet in his environment. The most important communication training is whispering. Try to move as close as possible to him. *Whisper*. At first, he may move away, but as he becomes more trusting he will allow you to whisper to him. You have made very significant progress when he allows you to whisper directly into his ear. Try to talk to him in whispers at every opportunity.

Many of these children act "deaf." You will wonder whether they are hearing anything. With persistence and with nonthreatening sounds they will often begin to allow some of your sound in.

We have noticed that, as these children begin to allow sound in, they begin to lose the ashen-gray pallor on their faces and they begin to have more facial color.

Hypoauditory

This child needs a great deal of auditory stimulation. It must not be chaotic stimulation. The sounds should be sharp, easily recognized, and should be given singly, not in combination.

The environment should be sound-reflective. Rugs, draperies, and acoustical tile should be kept to a minimum. Ceramic tile is excellent because of its reflective qualities. The kitchen and bathroom will be the most sound-fulfilling for this child. He should be allowed—in fact, encouraged— to spend considerable time each day in both rooms, experimenting with sound.

The sounds given as stimulation should be of a start-and-stop nature. They should not be constant and they should not be given in competition with a great deal of background noise, such as a musical background. The child should be given toys that make noise when they are being used. One toy manufacturer is well known for having made noisy toys for at least a generation.

The hypoauditory child will enjoy traffic noises and crowds. Be careful with him in traffic, because his ability to judge sound sources is inaccurate. Thus he will be in some danger in traffic.

He will use palpation and sonar-type bouncing of sound off objects to learn more about the sound component

of each object. He will do this with gusto. These loud, repetitive sounds are quite irritating to those of us with normal
hearing. Hence, each day he should be given a place to do
these things without interfering with the comfort of other
family members. During this daily period he should be allowed to bang and shout without incurring the wrath of
those around him.

Generally, he will love animals, especially dogs. Occasionally he might hurt the dog to hear the dog bark or growl.
At the outset, therefore, he must be carefully supervised
while playing with the dog in order to protect him from
the dog's reaction.

This youngster will love being at the seashore, to go shopping, or to live in a crowded, noisy camper. These areas all
increase the intensity of his sound environment.

He will profit from using sound magnifiers such as a
small microphone and amplifier set. He will also profit from
using a walkie-talkie. Don't force him to use these, but
merely teach him how they work.

In addition to sound magnification, he needs sound
storage. A simple cassette tape recorder will help him to
store sounds to replay to himself.

Do all that you can to help him to understand sounds, to
be able to locate them, to be able to store them.

Do lots of talking in a firm, loud voice. Talk in sentences to him about the world about him. Try to get his
attention to your words, but *don't force his attention.*

Auditory—White Noise

Do not permit this child to have too much time for just
sitting and listening to himself. Keep at him constantly with
sounds, especially speech. He must be kept busy doing all
kinds of chores and activities to distract him from hearing
his inner sounds.

Snow often frightens him, as will walking in snow. It is too quiet. He often will become quite agitated during times of barometric changes. Often his behavior will predict storms. Prior to the arrival of a storm his behavior will grow increasingly agitated. The change in barometric pressure seems to make some change in his internal noises.

Cats are good pets. Often this child may listen to the cat's purring, or inner noise.

Encourage odd balance positions such as lying on the floor, standing on his head, rocking with his eyes closed, or running. All of these activities change his inner sounds and will help him to begin to differentiate among his inner sounds. Try to join in these activities and try to control them through touch.

The next step is to help him learn to distinguish between internal and external sounds. Show him sound-producing toys. Be sure you show him where sounds originate, in every instance. Have him feel sound-producing objects, such as speakers, pianos, washing machines (both clothes and dish) and radios—to learn about sound vibration through his hands.

Discourage and delete from his environment constant background noises, such as continually running air conditioners. Delete any sound that is constant, such as the sound of the surf at the seashore. He will have great difficulty differentiating these as "outside" or "inside" sounds.

Buy him a good stethoscope so that he can listen to his heart, his blood circulation (particularly at his neck), and his digestion. Periodically interrupt this and gently lift the stethoscope. Talk into it. Be sure he sees your mouth and feels your breath when you speak into the stethoscope.

Discourage constant sounds from him, such as humming or constant tapping. If he breathes hard (hyperventilates) and listens to himself, have him listen with the stethoscope. In general, try to discourage the hyperventilation.

Play many "sound" games, the goal of which is to teach him that they are *"outside"* sounds that should be heard. Be sure he uses his eyes and watches you as you produce the sound. Repetition is very important and very helpful in teaching this child.

TASTE

These children present feeding problems. Some of them (hyper) present such problems of food intake that their health may become affected. The others (hypo) are truly dangerous to themselves because they tend to eat anything and everything they see. They must be carefully supervised. Dangerous materials or liquids should not be allowed in their homes.

Remember that the tip of the tongue is the most sensitive tactilely and that it is also our most-used taste discriminator. It deals primarily with sweet and salt tastes. The sides of the tongue deal with sour, and the back with bitter.

Hypertaste

These are the feeding problems. They will gag if food is given to them that is too tasteful. Bland foods with no spices are indicated.

Since these youngsters tend to use the tips of their tongues, sweet and salt tastes are familiar to them. *Do not use sour or bitter* in their foods until the children have normalized their taste.

Never give these children carbonated drinks, because the carbonation tends to increase the taste effect of the drink.

Be certain that the bland foods that these children are

served are of the most nutritious kind. Small appetites are characteristic of these children. They will not eat a large quantity of any food.

When feeding them, give them a new food mixed with some familiar food that you know they will accept. When he is ready for some practice, take a tiny drop of some new bland food and put it on the roof of his mouth, right behind his front teeth. Take another drop and put it on the tip of his tongue. Now tell him what the food is.

As he learns to tolerate this procedure with bland foods, move on to some sweet and then salt tastes. Remember, only a small drop behind the upper teeth, then a drop on the tip of the tongue, and then tell him what the taste is.

With patience you can work up to sours and bitters such as vinegar and mustard. Be sure to start with the bland tastes and to proceed slowly to the salty and sweet. Use sour and bitter tastes last.

Hypotaste

First of all, remove from the house *all* potentially poisonous materials, such as cleaning agents, strong soaps, kerosene, etc. Because this child has poor ability to discriminate taste, he is dangerous to himself. He will be satisfied to eat anything you give him or that he discovers for himself, at times including nonedible substances. You must be careful that he eats a balanced diet.

Since he has no taste discrimination, he must be taught. With this child we have found that it is easiest to start with the *back* of the tongue, using bitter tastes. Give him bitter tastes in liquid form. Tell him what it is, then have him taste it. Do bitter tastes only in a fluid form for approximately two weeks. Then proceed to sour tastes. These are also best introduced in liquid form. We have found that the fluid in a sour pickle contains a good sour taste. Place a few drops on each *side* of the tongue and show him the pickle container. Let him smell the container. Tell him it is sour and that these are sour pickles. Do this for about two weeks. Next introduce salt tastes, *on the tip of the tongue,* then two weeks of sweet tastes—also on the tip of the tongue. Each daily taste training session should include from four to eight applications of tastes. For each application, a few drops will suffice. When you have completed the sweet tastes, go back and start again with bitter tastes. *Always place the taste on the part of the tongue indicated above.*

When, in this way, the child has learned about the tastes, you can begin to mix up the applications—one day sweet, one day bitter, one day sour, one day salty. Following success with this mixture, you can mix the tastes during the applications within the same day.

Taste—White Noise

This child constantly has a taste in his mouth. It is an inner taste, which captures his attention. He tastes his own saliva and, as a result, sucks his own tongue or just sits tasting his own saliva.

Discourage his regurgitating and rechewing his food as much as you possibly can. Often his tongue will have become thick due to his sucking. Try to get him to exercise his tongue. With clean hands, pull out his tongue and massage it. When you brush his teeth, be sure you also brush his tongue, both top and sides, being careful not to brush the tongue too long at any time so as not to irritate it. Some children react well to a mouth irrigator containing a fairly strong mouthwash. Be careful to prevent the child from swallowing the mouthwash.

When the child is ready, you can begin to break through

the "white noise." First, take a food representative of one of the four tastes (e.g., a sugar cube) and place it in the space between his teeth and his cheek. See that he does not chew it. As it dissolves, its taste will gradually seep toward his tongue. Do this for all four tastes. Find the taste he tolerates best when it is presented in this manner.

For training, start with that taste. Be sure you show him what it is, let him smell it, then place it between his teeth and cheek, allowing it to dissolve. After a week of this technique, move on to another of the four tastes. Remember, he is to allow it to melt in his mouth between his teeth and cheek. Be sure you tell him what each taste is before you place it in his mouth. This can be done from four to eight times, daily.

If he does not tolerate the bitter or sour tastes, use a food that has only a trace of sour or bitter in its taste makeup, such as cooked fruit with lemon juice or cooked chopped-up bitter endive. When the child has learned to tolerate these tastes, begin to teach him to differentiate tastes by presenting them to him and telling him what they are. Always begin with sweet and salty, and always (for "white noise") begin the training with the tip of the tongue. As you train him, introduce those tastes into his food. Be sure that he chews his food. Discourage food gulping because he is not properly tasting his food, and food-gulping children often regurgitate and rechew their food, a process that you should always discourage.

Repetition is very helpful and very important in teaching this child.

VISION

Be cognizant of all light and light sources when considering the visual child. Also, observe all movement in which the eyes are involved. This includes total body movement, movement of arms and legs within the field of vision, and looking at moving objects, such as compulsive train or traffic-watching, or watching spinning objects.

It also includes all forms of rhythmic movement—jumping and rocking—where the eyes are involved. Spinning is commonly used visually by these children.

Look for all sticks, rubber bands, or toys that are manipulated rhythmically in front of the eyes. In short, watch the behavior and determine what behavior is carried out in the field of vision and for the benefit of the eyes.

Hypervision

With these children we must diminish the gross visual stimulation as much as possible. They do best in a subdued visual environment, with indirect lighting and subdued wall colors. Watch for bright or flashing lights and be sure that they are eliminated. Also eliminate from his environment mirrors and other shiny objects with which he can disperse or play with light.

Do not force him to be on the seashore on bright days. The amount of light plus its reflection tend to confuse him.

Take him outdoors in the evening, when the sun has gone down and when shadows are not so sharp. An automobile ride on a bright day can be harrowing, with its constantly changing light and shadow. Have him use sunglasses if he must be outdoors in the sun or must go for a sun-filled automobile ride.

The parent must gain control of the movement of light. Hold a small penlight in your hand and move it about the room, having his eyes follow the light as you control its motion. If he is a spinner of objects, *you* spin them and stop them. If he is a body spinner, *you* spin his body for him.

Discourage all visual activity that *he* controls, in favor of visual activity controlled from outside himself.

Give him intricate visual tasks to do, such as puzzles and tracing. At the outset, help him do these tasks.

Begin to teach him to read. Surprisingly, these children learn to read quickly and read quite well. We often see these children read extremely well, even though they have not learned to speak and even though they seem to spend only a tiny amount of attention on what is presented to them.

These children tend to have phenomenal visual memories. In the past some have considered them "idiots savants." They can look at an intricate visual pattern, such as a page of reading, and remember it almost photographically. Do not allow the child to spend too much of his time at one type of visual task. Constantly *vary* the kinds of visual tasks you give him. Increase their complexity as rapidly as he will tolerate.

Hypovision

This child requires a great deal of sunlight, bright lights in a brightly painted room, and general visual stimulation. Contrast of light and dark are important, as is the sharpness of shadows. Lighting should be direct, not subdued.

Be careful of stairs and heights with this child. Also beware of traffic, but have him spend a good deal of time outdoors. Gray, cloudy days sometimes disturb him.

Be sure you encourage him to feel everything he sees. Teach him through show-and-tell technique. Show him things, talk about them, let him feel them, and then move around the room so that he sees them at varying distances and in varying lights.

Use different-colored lights and use shadows to teach

him. Show him how shadows change when an object is moved in relation to the light source.

Keep a constant check on his activity. Does he see what you see? Keep reminding him to look at things and to feel them.

Buy him a large magnifying glass with which he can look at the world.

Discourage him from looking at the sun or directly into light sources. He must look at things and people who are bathed in light and not at the light sources. He must learn that light has no meaning by itself, but to have meaning, light must be related to objects and people.

Since both people and objects have *fuzzy edges* for this child, he will often have difficulty pouring fluids, placing things where he wants them, or picking up things. Help him to learn about edges of people and objects. Have him feel them, look at them, then feel them again.

Motion is a problem for this child, for it further complicates his fuzzy-edged world. Teach him to walk toward an object while looking at it. Then have him feel it.

Occasionally such a child will indicate that he sees an aura around an object or a person. What he is seeing is a fuzzy edge or a hazy outline of the object. This happens most often when it is an object that falls out of the center of his visual field. Objects or people seen off at the side of his visual field have hazier and fuzzier edges for him than do those in his center of vision. When training him, make sure that he looks at the object straight on, in the center of his visual field, and not from the side.

Buy him a box of fluorescent crayons. Draw pictures with them and show him the pictures in the dark. Draw a crayon line on the edges of his furniture in his room so that he can see the outlines of his furniture at night.

Vision—White Noise

This child's vision operates as though it were turned inward to himself. We must help him to look outward to the world.

You must discourage any touching, tapping, or rubbing of the eyes, because through these activities the child is giving himself visual stimulation from within. He creates flashes of light and light displays in his brain by tapping or rubbing his own eyes.

He will be helped by having you play with a penlight that *you* control. The light must go on and off a great deal, but *you*, not the child, must control the light.

Don't try to force eye contact, having him look at you. Start with toys that have lights and a penlight, in a semidarkened room. *You* must control the light source. *You* must gain his visual attention. Show him the light source —but *don't allow him to manipulate the source*. Start with light and dark, then move quickly into colors.

Use a brightly lighted mirror to help him see what is outside his vision. You must not only gain his visual attention, it must be visual attention *toward* something controlled from the outside. Have him practice in a semidark, quiet room. Move around him; don't allow him to pay attention at one distance or in one direction only. Constantly vary both distance and direction.

For this child objects and people are, at times, surrounded by a *flicker*. As a result, their constancy is threatened for him. His own movement will seem to take place in jumps, not in the smooth motion that we see. As a result of the tendency to flicker and the tendency to see smooth movements as jerky movements, the child becomes easily discouraged with the outside visual world and returns to his own inner visual world.

Use a brightly lighted floor-length mirror, lighted prefer-
ably with natural light. As he sees himself in the mirror,
trace the outline of his body on the mirror with your finger.
Point to different parts of his body in the mirror. Have
him point to the parts of your body.

Have him spend a good deal of time watching you in
motion in the mirror. Make your motions exaggeratingly
smooth. Now, have him walk, creep, and move his arms
slowly while watching himself in the mirror. Be sure that
everything is done smoothly so that he learns that motion
can be seen as smooth and not jerky.

Don't allow him to spend much time at his old habit of
looking inward. Discourage the habit and replace it with a
visual world at which he must look and to which he must
pay attention.

Repetition is very helpful and very important in teaching
this child.

These suggestions for achieving the survival stage are
not, and cannot be, all-inclusive. They are a guide only,
since every child is different. If, however, you understand
the problem, and you understand the approach, you can
generalize and *improvise*. The goal is to normalize the affected sensory channel, as far as possible, in order to reduce the rhythmic behavior that steals the child's attention
away from the real world.

Remember, he is trying to normalize his own abnormal
sensory channel or channels. Help him. He has been trying, alone, to help himself. You can assist him. This as-
sistance is, at best, *symptomatic* treatment. These
suggestions are aimed at helping the child to rid himself
of his aberrant behavioral symptoms. Only if these symptoms are decreased will he be able to survive long enough
to move on to the next stage.

Those children who succeed at the survival stage exhibit very significant changes in behavior. As a result, the culture can begin to tolerate them. In addition, those children who succeed in the survival stage can enter the next stage with the supreme ability to pay attention. They developed this ability during their presurvival stage.

When the child has achieved the survival stage, he can be viewed as a brain-injured child who has difficulty with communication and speech. He can then begin central treatment.

X
TREATING THE CAUSE

In the past, psychiatric intervention was the usual approach to treating autistic children. Today, there is general agreement that psychiatric intervention has not succeeded with these children as a group. Unsuccessful treatment is usually followed by institutional placement.

In 1971 Dr. Kanner[1] reported on a follow-up study of the eleven autistic children about whom he first reported in the original article about autism. In those early years there was little treatment. Many went to institutions. Kanner, in retrospect, feels that institutional placement tended to cause in the patients a complete retreat to near nothingness. His follow-up report indicates that not much progress has been made in treatment during those three decades. No treatment has surfaced that could be called a successful form of treatment during those years.

There is general agreement in the field that the search for new treatment must continue and that the treatments

[1] Kanner, L. A., "A Follow-up Study of Eleven Autistic Children Originally Reported in 1943." *Journal of Autism and Childhood Schizophrenia,* I(2):119–45 (1971).

tried in the past have very little to offer. It is also obvious that treatment must be central in nature.

Central treatment is treatment that is aimed at the *cause* of the problems and not merely at the symptoms. Central treatment must in some way change the structure, development, or organization of the behavior and of the child. There are a number of central or quasicentral approaches becoming available to parents. There is a great deal of controversy surrounding each of them.

The primary cause of the controversy is the fact that there is no agreement as to the cause of autism. There continues to be the conflict between the psychogenic and the organic school of thought as to cause. In addition, there is no agreement within either of those categories as to the most successful approach.

Another reason for the controversy is that no single approach has all the answers; each has its successes and its failures. Parents have learned to seek out the approach that seems most reasonable to them and that offers the most opportunity for their child. Parents have become increasingly sophisticated and more questioning; hence, if one approach doesn't succeed for their child, they seek another. Parents are no longer content to accept authoritarian direction; they now are making their decision on the basis of more knowledge and on the basis of results.

New treatment approaches are being developed. Some are attempting to treat not only the symptoms but are also attempting to treat what their proponents consider the basic cause of the problem.

All of these new approaches generate considerable controversy. The controversy starts with the goal of treatment. Heretofore, the very attempt to change the nervous system in any significant way short of surgery has been considered an unrealistic goal. Merely to attempt to change the function, structure, or organization of the human nervous system was to invite criticism. Until the decade of the sixties these were considered impossible goals, and since that time only a minority of the medical-educational Establishment have learned to consider these as possible and feasible goals.

These are the most commonly used approaches, which have as at least part of their goals an attempt to change the child in basic ways:

1. Behavior Modification

Basic to this approach is the concept of stimulus-response conditioning. Under this premise, the conditioning process is considered an imprinting process. That is, the process of conditioning physically modifies the nervous system. As conditioning takes place, it writes its memory traces in the white myelin covering of the nerve tissue. These are considered the long-term results of conditioning. In addition, the behavior modification proponents feel that short-term results are enhanced by re-enforcement through the punishment and/or reward applied. Some use only positive re-enforcement in the form of rewards such as hugging, candy, tokens of food, etc.

Whenever a child does something well, he is rewarded, the theory being that he will repeat the act because it was re-enforced, positively. Others stress negative re-enforcement. This group punishes poor performance or behavior with negative reactions—for example, electric shock, hitting, shouting, or taking things away. If what follows an act is unpleasant, the child will tend not to repeat that act, and thus the theory is that conditioning will set in.

Another basic premise of this approach is generalization. This is based on the theory that if a child learns specific facts and skills under the conditioning and/or re-enforcement circumstances, he will, as a result, learn how to learn. In essence, he will be able to generalize what he has learned in specific circumstances—to learning from life.

There is considerable controversy surrounding this approach. Some call it a dehumanizing approach because one will is forced upon another. The critics feel that this form of training, through forceful manipulation of both rewards and punishment, taking from the child his own choice of action, is too much like the procedures used in training animals. Others criticize it because they feel that it can only deal with symptoms—and somewhat insignificant symptoms, at that. They feel that the important human functions required for success in life are too complex and cannot be broken down into the kind of specifics that can be taught through behavior modification.

2. Education

This approach generally takes the form of "special education." Many different kinds of educational techniques exist under the umbrella of special education.

One theory is that fewer children in the class, coupled with more innovative teaching materials and teachers, will help these children to learn more effectively.

A second aspect is that the goals should be tailored to the child's needs. This tailoring would reduce the frustration that is the result of a more demanding educational program.

Another consideration is the provision of other children and the opportunity for socialization with other children with similar problems. With added opportunity for socialization and contact with others, this theory's proponents feel the child will develop emotionally and socially.

This approach also provides considerable opportunity for repetition in learning and for some perceptual training. Visual perception is taught through tracing, feeling lines and letters with fingers, etc.

Auditory perception is taught through an analytic approach to learning. The sounds of words are broken down alphabetically or linguistically into word families. The theory is that if the child learns to perceive the basic parts of wholes, he will have the tools for perceiving wholes and for learning. This approach is usually a school-based or tutorial approach.

There is considerable controversy surrounding the educational approach. One area of criticism is the goal. Critics feel that the educational approach is not a central approach, that it is instead the passing of knowledge with very little effect on the child. In essence, it is dealing with symptoms only. The other basic criticism is based on education's poor past performance. Special education and special educational techniques have not resulted in the hoped-for progress in children over the years. Because of the general disenchantment with special education, there is presently a strong move toward abolishing special classes and toward integrating those children considered special into the normal classes in an effort to produce more progress in these children.

3. Drugs

This approach attempts through drugs to "facilitate" the function of the nervous system. Some drugs have an *excitatory* effect on the nervous system and others have a *suppressive* effect. The proponents of drug use for brain-injured children feel that, through the use of certain drugs, the nervous system can be helped to operate more quickly in those children whose general performance is slow.

Through the use of other drugs they attempt to slow down those children who are hyperactive.

Some drugs used for excitation or suppression act directly upon the brain, others affect the neurones (the nerves), and others affect the synapses (where the nerve endings meet). Much research is being carried out, aimed at finding the effects of drugs, and new data emerge daily. The difficult area of research is not in the chemical analysis of the drugs but in the lack of knowledge of the function of the nervous system.

Many, in both education and medicine, are using stimulant drugs with brain-injured children, especially those with soft signs of brain injury and those who are hyperactive.

The mode of action of stimulant drugs on calming some hyperactive children is not clear. One theory is that the hyperactivity indicates that the child's nervous system is underaroused, as one might be in deep fatigue or as the result of sleep deprivation. This underarousal results in the child's inability to pay attention or to maintain attention to relevant stimuli. As a result, the child inattentively flits from one stimulus to another. The use of a stimulant in this case would increase the arousal state of the nervous system and, as a result, the child would become better able to pay attention to relevant stimuli and he would become better able to maintain this attention; his flitting from one stimulus to another, resulting in hyperactivity, would be decreased. Millichap and Fowler's research[2] indicates that the most effective stimulants include methylphenidate (Ritalin), amphetamines (Dexedrine and Benzadrine), and deonol (Deaner).

Much less common, but still used, are tranquilizing or

[2] Millichap, J. and Fowler, G., "Treatment of Minimal Brain Dysfunction Syndromes." *Pediatric Clinics of North America* 4:767–77 (1967).

suppressive drugs. These are used in an attempt to slow down the activity of the nervous system. The most generally used tranquilizing agents are chlordiazepoxide (Librium) and chlorpromazine (Thorazine). Some tranquilizing agents are used for specific aggressive and destructive types of behavior: Thioridazine, Mellaril. Others are used specifically for anxiety: Diphenhydramine, Benadryl.

Other drugs are being tried to see if there is one that is effective with autistic children. The drug L-Dopa has been tried on autistic children to see if it changed the clinical and behavioral symptoms. Thus far the results have shown changes in blood serotonin and in blood platelet counts, but there has been no significant change in behavior.[3]

The stimulant types of drugs are the most commonly used. Many hyperactive children are given stimulant-type drugs such as amphetamines. Various estimates place the number of hyperactive children being so treated in the United States at between 150,000 and 300,000.

There is considerable controversy surrounding drug use with children. At present there is an antidrug feeling among parents. Drug use in general is being questioned at many levels, including the federal government level.

The use of amphetamines to control the behavior of autistic, hyperkinetic or hyperactive (overactive) children seems to be an American phenomenon. This approach is rarely used in other nations. Periodically, one sees criticism by Europeans working in this field of the massive use of drugs to control the behavior of children in the United States. Implied in this criticism is that the massive use of drugs to control behavior leads to greater illicit use of

[3] Ritvo, E. *et al.*, "Effects of L-Dopa on Autism." *Journal of Autism and Childhood Schizophrenia* I(2):190–205 (1971).

drugs and to a national attitude that tolerates more experimentation in illicit drug use than it should.

Drugs have been called by their critics just another, albeit more simple, method of restraint. Some critics[4] feel that the conditions of many hyperkinetic children on whom drugs are used have been misdiagnosed and that in some cases schools are not using adequate educational techniques to solve the problems presented by such children. The schools are, in effect, using drugs as the easy method of keeping children quiet and manageable in their classrooms.

4. Diet and Nutritional Supplements

This treatment approach aims at improving the internal function of the entire body through improving its nutritional status. It seeks to provide the proper variety of nutritional elements that the body needs, and it seeks to provide them in relatively large amounts so the body can have the constant opportunity to use them.

Autistic children are very often feeding problems. When viewing a group of autistic children, one is often struck by their generally poor nutritional status. A number of the proponents of the diet and food supplement treatment feel that autistic children have atypical metabolism, especially with regard to vitamins, essential amino acids, and essential fatty acids. Their proposal is to increase the intake of these nutrients to a high enough level so that the body will use them.

Another assumption of this group is that if the body is not functioning properly, neither will the brain and nervous system. The aim is to give the brain the most ideal *inner*

[4] Kripner, S. *et al.*, "A Study of Hyperkinetic Children Receiving Stimulant Drugs." *Academic Therapy* 8(3):261–69 (1973).

environment in which to operate—a sound mind in a sound body, so to speak.

Linus Pauling[5] has started a school of thought called orthomolecular therapy, which proposes that the creation of the optimum molecular composition of the brain is a way to treat behavioral illness. The molecular environment within the body dictates the rate of chemical reaction within the body; hence it also dictates the rate of reaction of the brain.

The orthomolecular stance is that our general diet does not provide the optimum concentrations of nutrients required by the brain, and that the brain is more sensitive to the lack of proper concentration or to the fluctuation of the concentration of these vital substances than are other parts of the body. The theory proposes that these vital substances must be added through food supplements.

The diet supplements suggested are the B Complex vitamins, nicotinic acid (niacin), ascorbic acid (vitamin C), thiamine, pyridoxine, and folic acid. Other substances added are zinc ion, magnesium ion, uric acid, and L(+) glutamate.

Hoffer proposed a more specific nutritional approach to schizophrenia in 1957.[6] Since that time there has been a continuing controversy over the use of niacin (vitamin B3) in the treatment of schizophrenia.

Rimland[7] studied the reaction of 200 autistic children to dietary supplements. At the outset the children's diets

[5] Pauling, L., "Orthomolecular Psychiatry." *Science* 160:265–71 (1968).

[6] Hoffer, A. *et al.*, "Treatment of Schizophrenia with Nicotinic Acid and Nicotinamide." *Journal of Clinical and Experimental Psychopathology and Quarterly Review of Psychiatric Neurology* 18:181 (1957).

[7] Rimland, B., *High Dosage Levels of Certain Vitamins in the Treatment of Children with Severe Mental Disorders* (San Diego, Calif.: Institute for Child Behavior Research, 1968).

were supplemented daily with moderate amounts of B vitamins and 2000 mg. of vitamin C. Later, B6 (150 mg.), niacinamide (2000 mg.), and pantothenic acid were also added.

There were increases in appetite, more sociability, and some speech improvement. Adelle Davis[8] proposed that adding more protein, linoleic acid, vitamins A, D, and E, calcium, magnesium, and other minerals would have resulted in even greater improvement.

There is considerable controversy surrounding the diet and nutritional supplement approach. Much of the criticism comes from medical men who feel that many of the therapeutic claims made for specific vitamins have not been substantiated and that minimum daily requirements have not been established for some. Others feel that too little is known about the over-all function of many vitamins and that it is possible that heavy doses of vitamins may have a negative effect on the body. This controversy has progressed to the point that presently federal regulations are being drawn up to tighten the control of the manufacture and sale of vitamins.

5. Neurological Organization

In the past, brain growth was considered a static and irrevocable fact, dictated by genetics, completed and unchangeable at birth. If injured, it could not be changed because it was believed that one had his lifetime complement of brain cells at birth and that from there on the process could only be one of deterioration.

In essence, the brain was viewed as an organ encased in bone, one that couldn't be influenced except through injury or through surgery. The theory of neurological or-

[8] Davis, A., *Let's Have Healthy Children* (New York: Harcourt Brace Javanovich, 1972), p. 338.

ganization views the growth and organization of the brain very differently.

The theory and procedures of neurological organization were first introduced in 1959.[9] A number of books have been written by others, expanding the concept since that first introduction.[10] The concept of neurological organization provided a new view of the development and organization of the nervous system. It also provided a new view about the plasticity and sequential growth potential of the brain and the nervous system as they related to sensory experience.

The human nervous system is complex because it is the result of many millions of years of evolutionary trial and error. Each child must retrace much of that long evolutionary history in developing and organizing his own nervous system to the fullest. Each child must follow that essential *sequence* of experiences and development that has been laid down by his evolutionary heritage, developing first the more ancient and more primitive sections of his brain and moving sequentially to the evolutionarily more recent and more complex areas. Each child must retrace this progression from the primitive reflex levels of muscular function to the uniquely human functions of speech and cognition.

According to the theory of neurological organization, if one or more levels are skipped or slighted, the final development and organization will be lacking.

Opportunity is the keynote of this sequential development. When opportunity is taken from a child, he is cheated and, as a result, he slights a developmental stage,

[9] Delacato, C., *The Treatment and Prevention of Reading Problems* (Springfield, Ill.: Charles C Thomas, 1959).

[10] In the Bibliography see: Doman, LeWinn, Melton, Thomas, and Wolf.

or in more extreme circumstances, he skips that developmental stage. When this happens the child is not completely developed and may exhibit either mobility problems, learning problems, or coordinational problems, leading to speech problems, reading problems, or behavior problems.

This developmental and organizational sequence, which begins at birth, progresses vertically through the spinal cord, then through the brain stem and medulla, the midbrain (old brain) and up through the two hemispheres of the cortex (the outer covering of the forebrain). In human beings there is one final stage in this developmental progression. This is a lateral development wherein one hemisphere of the cortex becomes the language or dominant hemisphere of the brain. As a result of this uniquely human, final, lateral stage, man becomes the only creature who is completely one-sided—that is, right-handed, right-eyed, right-eared, and right-footed, or left-handed, left-eyed, left-eared, and left-footed. And only man has spoken and written symbolic language.

Within the concept of neurological organization, brain growth is viewed as a dynamic and ever-changing process. It can be stopped by severe brain injury or by a total elimination of sensory input; it can be slowed by a milder brain injury or by a diminution of sensory input. Most importantly, it can be speeded and enhanced by increasing the sensory input. There is general agreement that function or use determines the optimal structure of various parts of the body. A body used in constant lifting of heavy weight shows an obvious increase in the size of those muscles used; people who live at high altitudes in rarefied air develop larger than usual lung capacity; starving people tend to have smaller than normal stomachs; inactive people tend to have soft and underdeveloped bodies.

According to this theory, the same is true for the brain.

Used extensively, it grows in both organization and structure; with a lack of use it is poorly organized and doesn't develop to its full capacity.

Treatment is based on recapitulation. If a developmental stage has been missed or short-changed, we provide the child the opportunity to go through that experience again to see if he can profit from it by thoroughly re-experiencing it. We know that the brain can become better organized if the significant developmental milestones that have been skipped are retraced and re-experienced.

In essence, we take the children back to a function typical of a much younger age. We have them practice the related motor functions that *re-enforce* their sensory development. When they have mastered the lower-level stages, we lateralize them by making them all right-sided or all left-sided.

Based on this theory we evaluate the child's development, using the Doman-Delacato Developmental Profile, which is based upon the significant areas of development. These areas are subdivided into the sequential order and time schedule in which they appear in normal children. There are three major intake or sensory areas:

1. *Vision:* beginning at birth with a light reflex and progressing through seven stages to understanding writing.

2. *Hearing:* beginning at birth with a startle reflex and progressing through seven stages to understanding speech.

3. *Tactility:* beginning at birth with tactile withdrawal reflexes and progressing through seven stages to the ability to recognize two-dimensional objects through manual tactility.

The profile also contains three expressive areas, each of which also progress through seven developmental stages:

1. *Mobility:* beginning at birth with movement without

mobility progressing through seven stages to normal human walking.

2. *Manual function:* beginning at birth with a grasp reflex and progressing through seven stages to the ability to write.

3. *Language:* beginning at birth as the birth cry and progressing through seven stages to human speech.

Using the profile we can evaluate a child's level of neurological organization. We can see where his development places him in each of the six significant areas. We can see how he compares with other children of the same age. We can see which developmental stages he has skipped completely or which he has slighted.

Treatment consists of providing the child with the opportunity to go back and re-experience the stage in which he exhibits a weakness. For example: The progression from movement without mobility to walking goes through a period of crawling on the abdomen, then to creeping on the hands and knees, then walking using the arms to balance, then walking in a human fashion, which we call cross-pattern walking. Watching people walk, you will notice that the right arm and left leg move forward as a step is taken and that the left arm and right leg move together on the next step. The upper and lower limb are opposite to each other with each step, hence the name "cross-pattern."

If a child exhibits a problem at some level of this mobility scale he is given the opportunity to go back and relive and, thus, re-experience that level for short periods each day. As an example, such a child might be returned to the crawling or creeping stage each day for added practice at that level of development.

If there is severe enough brain injury present so that the child cannot carry out that function, we pattern him. Patterning involves having three adults moving the child's body in coordinated fashion through the motions of crawling or creeping. Since the child cannot do it himself, the patterners do it to him and for him. Although the child is not moving his own body through the required motions, his body and brain learn how it "feels" to go through the motions and how it feels to carry out the action. When he becomes able to do so on his own, through learning how it feels to do so, he is allowed to crawl or creep on his own.

As another example, consider the child on the visual pathway. To progress from having a light reflex at birth to reading, if he has not fully profited from the convergence level, and as a result cannot converge his two eyes together on a target, he must be given much opportunity to use his eyes together in a lifelike setting typical of that passed through by a much younger child. Although this is a developmental skill level that takes place prior to one year of age in normal children, the child is helped to recapitulate these experiences to see if he can profit from them the second time he goes through them.

In order to improve his chances of success at these recapitulated lower stages, we provide them for each individual child with increased *frequency, intensity,* and *duration,* always coupling them with the opportunity for the appropriate and re-enforcing motor activity. To accomplish this in practical terms, we have had to make our program a *home program.* We orient the parents completely and then have them carry out this developmental and organizational program at home.

But theoretical questions arise.

Does *use* change the development and organization of the brain? What is the role of increased frequency, intensity, and duration of stimulation to the brain? Does related motor activity re-enforce sensory function?

The answers to these questions require a dynamic view of brain development.

We know that disuse has a negative effect on the function of the brain.

Reisen showed that disuse of the visual system in baby monkeys produced blindness.[11] We know that this is true for other body systems. If we don't use our muscles, they atrophy. If we don't use our balance systems, they lose efficiency. If we don't use our cardiovascular system, such as in extended bed rest, its efficiency is curtailed.

There are other studies with animals that show that the way a brain is used, the way it is stimulated, has a significant effect on both its structure and chemical activity.

Klosovskii in Russia studied cats from the same litter. He placed half the litter of cats on a small rotating device when they were twenty-four to thirty-six hours old. The other half of the litter was allowed a normal life.

Those on the rotating device were rocked back and forth for a number of hours per day. The theory being tested was that if the brain develops through use, this rocking activity would increase the size of the balance centers of their brains.

After ten to nineteen days of rotating them, he sacrificed the cats and found that they showed 22 to 35 percent greater increase in the *size* of the balance areas when their brains were compared with those of their brothers and sisters who served as controls.[12]

At the University of California in Berkeley, a group of scientists headed by David Krech studied the plasticity and growth of the brain. They found that when mice are stimu-

[11] Reisen, A. H., "Effects of Stimulus Deprivation on the Development and Atrophy of the Visual Sensory System." *American Journal of Orthoptics* 30:23–26 (1960).

[12] For an excellent description of this and other similar studies, see Klosovskii, B. N., *The Development of the Brain and its Disturbance by Harmful Factors* (New York: Macmillan, 1962).

lated through their senses, their brains grow larger and weigh more than those of their littermates who have not been so stimulated. They found that when vision is stimulated, there is a great increase in the size and weight of the visual areas of the brain compared to the nonstimulated group. The same thing happened in experiments on rats. Given an environment that contained more sensory stimulation, the rats developed a greater weight and thickness of brain tissue and an increase in the brain's chemical activities.

There are also studies that show that motor reenforcement has a very significant effect on brain organization. Richard Held of M.I.T. conducted some ingenious studies of development. He brought up littermate kittens in darkness, allowing them to see only during the experiment. One kitten was placed in a basket with his head uncovered and his legs sticking out and touching the floor, so that he could turn the basket around by using his legs. The other kitten was placed in a basket with only his head uncovered so that he could see, but he couldn't move his legs. His basket was connected to the first by a pulley so that, when the first kitten moved, the second moved in the same direction and traveled the same distance. The only difference was that one kitten's legs were touching the floor and turning the basket and the other kitten's legs were not being used at all. Held found that the kitten that was allowed to use his legs to create movement learned to see and to perceive. The other kitten, who had the identical visual experience but who did not have the motor experience of moving his legs, remained unable to see effectively.

These are the theoretical bases of neurological organization. The brain develops and is organized through use. The brain develops through significant developmental milestones from birth on. If one or more of these milestones is missed completely, or is only partially developed, the organization of the nervous system will be lacking. Where we find the child lacking, we have him go back to recapitulate those functions of an earlier age, with increased frequency, intensity, and duration, providing constant opportunity for motor re-enforcement. Through this recapitulation we give him the opportunity to further organize and develop his nervous system.

In addition to theory there must be treatment and the results of treatment. In addition there must be other empirical evidence replicating the treatment and replicating the results.

Neurological organization, as a diagnostic and treatment rationale, has been used and its results have been replicated by a wide variety of specialists working with a wide variety of children. Since the concept was first introduced in 1959 it has been used in the treatment of very severely brain-injured children, moderately and mildly injured children, through to children with learning, reading, and behavior problems with much success. It has been found to be significantly effective in the treatment of severely brain-injured children whose primary problem was lack of mobility.[13] Neurological organization has resulted in significantly greater gains for such children when those gains have been compared with the gains made by like children under different systems of treatment.[14]

A highly publicized controlled study was conducted by the National Association for Retarded Children during 1972, and the results were made public in 1973. The children treated and compared in this study were mildly to

[13] Doman, R.; Spitz, E.; Zucman, E.; Delacato, C.; and Doman, G., "Children with Severe Brain Injury—Neurological Organization in Terms of Mobility." *Journal of the American Medical Association* 174:257–62 (1960).

[14] Wolf, J., *Results of Treatment in Cerebral Palsy* (Springfield, Ill.: Charles C Thomas, 1968).

moderately retarded state school residents. This study compared the effectiveness of a modified program of neurological organization with a physical activity and recreation group and also with a no-treatment group. The National Association for Retarded Children reported that the results achieved with the modified neurological organization group, which they called the sensorimotor group, were of such significant positive benefit that this treatment approach should be recognized as one of the approaches to be used in the treatment of children with the appropriate handicaps.

Ten independent studies were conducted, two of which were doctoral dissertations, to assess the effectiveness of neurological organization in treating reading problems.[15] These studies showed consistently greater improvements in reading performance in the groups where neurological organization was used to treat the reading problems than was made by the control groups being treated by other methods.

After the autistic child has passed through the survival stage, he can be treated as a brain-injured child. The brain injury is the central cause of his problem. Parents at this point must seek a treatment approach aimed at modifying the nervous system, where the problem started and where the problem still exists. There are a number of central or quasicentral approaches. There will, no doubt, be more in the future. Each of these approaches produces successes and failures. The parent must seek that approach that is the most effective for his child. The final evaluation should be: Has this approach brought my child closer to integration into society? If an approach fails, parents will seek another. If it succeeds, parents will know.

[15] Delacato, C., *Neurological Organization and Reading* (Springfield, Ill.: Charles C Thomas, 1966).

XI
"THEORIES ARE THEORIES"

I once heard it said that theories are like women—it is better that they be fertile than that they be good. Of the two descriptions, my hope is that *fertility* might be the more apt for this theory. If this theory creates new ways of looking at children, if it creates more search and research, then its fertility will be assured.

In 1966 the *Medical World News* stated that no one can ever guess how many autistic children there are. One might question why a relatively rare behavioral problem deserves so much attention. First, many feel, and I concur, that there are more of these children than had been suspected. Second, their extremely poor prognosis and their historical failure to respond to classical treatment have led to their abandonment. As a result, they represent a significant challenge. And third, if we understand these children who represent the most extreme form of behavior aberration, perhaps we can begin to understand better the lesser problems of behavior that surround us. These children can teach us so much, not only about other children with lesser problems, but also about *all* children—and in the end, perhaps, about behavior in general.

The basic premise of my theory is that these problems are *not* psychological but that they are organic—specifically, neurologically caused. *These children are not psychotic. They are brain-injured.* The brain injury causes perceptual problems, and so the real world is distorted on its complex journey from the receptor (eye, ear, skin, tongue, nose) to the brain. Their aberrant behavior is their attempt to normalize the affected sensory system.

For too long the human brain has kept its secrets hidden from us. Modern technology, coupled with more rigorous and more creative research by many in the field, is beginning to expose these hidden secrets to the glare of science. In the past, when we could find no organic relationships to a disease or a behavior, there was no choice but to look to the psychological, which Freud had exposed a century ago. With new neurological information emerging daily, perhaps we will gain a greater understanding of what in the past had been considered emotional illness.

When one proposes a new theory, one is comforted if there are others who are at least in partial agreement. One is even more comforted if there are others working toward the same theory. Bergman and Escalona described unusual sensitivities and perceptual distortions resulting from an inadequate stimulus barrier. They proposed that ordinary stimuli might be overwhelming to the autistic child.[1] Shevrin and Toussieng proposed that inadequate tactile sensation, either through an exceptionally high stimulus barrier or maternal understimulation, or through a very low stimulus barrier, or through overstimulation by the mother, were

[1] Bergman, P. and Escalona, S., "Unusual Sensitivities in Very Young Children." *Psychoanalytical Studies of Children* 3–4:333–52 (1949).

significant etiological factors in autism.[2] Schopler wrote
about the development, or lack of development, of near
and far receptors as factors in autism.[3] Rimland (1964)
stated that autistic children suffer an impairment in the
integration between sensory intake and memory. He suggests that the reticular activating system is the site of the
lesion.[4]

"Other authors: Anderson, 1952; Bakwin, 1953; Bender,
1942; Chapman, 1957; Easton, 1962; Fish, 1960; Gold-
stein, 1959; Mahler, 1955; Pasamanick and Knoblock,
1963; Soddy, 1963; White, De Meyer, and De Meyer, 1964
suggest that at least some autistic and schizophrenic children may have defective nervous or other somatic regula-
tory systems."[5] Ornitz and Ritvo (1968) state that the
inconstancy of perceptual integration is the fundamental
cause of early developmental failure of self to nonself differentiation.[6]

A most recent and inclusive book on the subject is *Infantile Autism: Concepts, Characteristics, and Treatment,*
edited by Michael Rutter and published in 1971 by Williams and Wilkins, of Baltimore. It is a conference report
of a group of leaders in the field. Through reading this book
one can see the gradual change in thinking that has taken
place. Autism is increasingly considered a problem of cog-

[2] Shevrin, H. and Toussieng, P., "Conflict over Tactile Experience in
Emotionally Disturbed Children." *Journal of American Academy of Child
Psychiatry* 1:564–90 (1962).

[3] Schopler, E., "Early Infantile Autism and the Receptor Process."
Archives of General Psychiatry 13:327–37 (1965).

[4] Rimland, B., *Infantile Autism: The Syndrome and Its Implication
for a Neural Theory of Behavior* (New York: Appleton-Century-Crofts,
1964).

[5] Churchill, I.; Alpern, G.; and De Meyer, M., *Infantile Autism*
(Springfield, Ill.: Charles C Thomas, 1971), p. 30.

[6] Ornitz, E. and Ritvo, E., "Perceptual Inconstancy of Early Infantile
Autism." *Archives of General Psychiatry* 18:76–98 (1968).

nition or language disorder, probably resulting from sensory-motor dysfunction. This collection of papers moves the problem away from the purely psychogenic and closer to the sensory and brain-injury stance. As an example, it points out that more than one fourth of autistic children develop a convulsive disorder, a generally recognized sign of brain injury. It also points up the fact that the prognosis for these children remains quite poor. Most important, it points up the fact that the "search" for real answers is varied and continues.

There were others sharing new insights. Veras had been so very correct at the outset, when he encouraged me to reread Ardrey, Morris, and Lorenz. They helped the field of ethology to mature and to be heard. Through their studies of man's origins, they concluded that *man had instinctive drives for hunting, exploration, and territory.* These instincts helped to make man what he is.

These four men—Dart, Ardrey, Morris, and Lorenz— are the pioneers. They are the spokesmen of a new kind of investigation. These men help us to understand ourselves and our children, through focusing on our origins. Their delineation of instinctive behavior, their search for universal behaviors and causes in animals, including man, have given a new impetus to man's favorite activity—that of trying to understand himself. *Each of their generalizations relates to the autistic child.*

Man is a hunter. I must agree that man is, indeed, an instinctive hunter. But the quarry for modern man is not food, it is *sensation,* needed for the development of his nervous system. The nervous system develops through use. When man can't find enough sensory nourishment for his nervous system, he becomes frustrated and his behavior degenerates. Yes, we are all hunters—not of food, but of sensation.

The autistic child is the most addicted and the most frustrated hunter of all. He must hunt to live. But his hunting is for the peculiar sensory experience that he needs. The rest of us hunt sensations. When we have bagged our quarry, we enjoy it and move on to the next quarry. These children, because of their brain injury, are not satisfied by their quarry. They must continue to hunt the same sensations, over and over. They are locked in. They are never satiated. We must unlock them from their sensory addictions before they can become able to move beyond their injury. We must help them in their hunt, help them to use sensation more normally, and then to move on to the next level of hunting.

It is almost as though we have to help them to learn to profit from their hunting, to digest the product of their hunt, to be nourished by it, and then to move on to new hunting grounds.

Another generalization is that man is extremely inquisitive and, as a result, he is a consummate explorer. I must agree with the ethologists that man is *instinctively an explorer*. But I feel that we are not explorers because we are inquisitive—we are explorers because we are *acquisitive*. We are avid for sensation that meets our needs in terms of frequency, intensity, duration, and variability. This constant activity (which at times becomes hyperactivity) has as its goal the acquisition of newer and more sensation. Sensation is the nutriment of the brain and its force for change.

Indeed, today we see a new industry being born: the *experience industry*. Man no longer is satisfied to be a casual tourist or spectator of the world. He insists on being *involved* in experiencing through his entire sensory apparatus all that goes on about him. As a result, he acquires these sensory imprints in his brain, to be stored forever.

This is man's ultimate activity. It involves his survival. Without these acquisitions, without these imprints, the brain does not develop. Without them, man's brain would never have evolved and we would have become prisoners within our own bodies.

The autistic child explores constantly, but his unreliable sensory system creates many difficulties. As a result, the autistic child explores only what he can control. He does not venture into new areas because he is fearful. Because of his unreliable sensory system, he attempts to control completely the sensations with which his brain is to deal. His unreliable sensory system makes all incoming stimulation ambiguous. One of the brain's primary functions is to create some semblance of order out of the chaos of sensation surrounding us. Because of the ambiguity fed to his brain by an unreliable sensory system, the autistic child cannot establish this order. Because of his unreliable sensory system, he can only store ambiguous sensory data. But he supersedes these problems. Since he has no control of the sensory system, he chooses to control the inputs going into the sensory system. He allows *in* those that he alone controls; the others are rejected as chaos. As a result, he remains mired at one level of sensory function.

I must agree with the ethologists that space and territory acquisition are instinctive needs. To most of us space and territory are constants, which are finite, measurable and, therefore, understandable and protectable. This is not the case with the autistic child. For him space and territory are *not constant*. They are ambiguous; they represent not safety, but extreme danger.

Children who have hypersensory systems, or parts of systems, suffer from a distortion of space. Space is constantly *crowding* them as a result of their hypersensory problem. Space becomes so crowding, so close that it becomes overwhelming and it renders them incapable of functioning. To these children territory is not an instinctive need, it is an enemy. It is an enemy which, because of their hypersensory system, crowds them, constantly impinges on them, and stifles them, so much so that they cannot pay attention to anything else.

The hyposensory child's sense of space and territory is also distorted, but the distortion is all of an *expanding* nature. Space and territory become terrifyingly vast because of this distortion. These children are unable to control any space because of the sensory distortion. Space becomes an elusive enemy without constancy, without boundaries and, as a result, without reality. Here again territory is not an instinctive need; it is the enemy.

Man is the product of his evolution. If we agree with Ardrey that we are risen apes (as contrasted to Rousseau's belief that we are fallen angels), we must study the nature of the ladder upon which we rose. What changed? The only real change was in the size and complexity of man's brain and nervous system. And it grew—through use. If there is interference or injury, use is difficult. Without use, there is no growth.

Because of the brain injury, autistic children hunt, explore, and use space and territory in a very different fashion from all other animals, including other humans. They do not follow the behavioral rules of an instinctive nature, which all animals must follow if they are to survive.

They not only do not follow the *learned patterns of behavior* that we expect of children, *they do not even follow the ancient instinctive patterns of behavior because of their perceptual dysfunction. This is why they are considered so very alien. This is why they are constantly threatened with abandonment.* They break all of the rules, even the ancient instinctive rules common to the entire animal world. Their distorted sensory systems create for them a distorted world, and they choose to become prisoners inside themselves rather than deal with a frightening, ever-changing and, above all, seemingly hostile world.

Without a change in their distorted perceptual systems, they are destined to remain prisoners within their own bodies. With change, with less distortion, with less ambiguity of what arrives at their brains, there is a hope that they can be released from their prisons.

This theory is not presented as a "cure-all." Even with this theory and these practices, I have failures. Some fail to reach the survival stage, while others reach it and then fail at the central treatment stage. But in a field where we are grasping and searching for answers, in a field where failure is the rule, each small or large step forward becomes important.

Hopefully, my ideas will help a greater number of these autistic children to survive. By surviving I mean that we can change their behavior enough at the outset so that the culture will not attempt to abandon or institutionalize such children. If these youngsters can be helped through the survival stage, we have gained time and a new opportunity to help them toward fuller lives and perhaps toward eventual integration.

To others working in the field I say, "We are still in the 'search' stage." More and more attempts must, and will, be made to help these autistic children—first, to survive, then hopefully to integrate. Theories are tools. We set them up, then try to refine, prove, or disprove them. We learn in the process. As a result, we look at the problem in different ways.

Hopefully, those who follow will refine, restate, and improve on what I have found. But in the end what matters is the improvement of autistic children. As more light is shed on the problem, as more people become concerned, as more communication takes place, hopefully we will find not only better understanding, but also more effective treatment. And if our understanding of these children increases, perhaps some day in the future we will become able to accept the ultimate challenge: that of preventing the problem.

XII
CASE MATERIALS

These cases have been selected to illustrate the concepts of this theory. To avoid misunderstanding or confusion I have included only children who had been diagnosed as autistic by some outside, qualified professional person prior to our first seeing them. Each of these children was labeled autistic by at least one professional prior to the time their parents sought their first appointment with us.

These children followed a home program carried out by their parents. We first saw each child and his parents for a one-week evaluation and parent-orientation period. The parents then went home with their child to execute the program we had outlined. At two- or three-month intervals they returned with their children for re-evaluation, program changes, and new instructions. Each re-evaluation required one full day.

CASE S.

(Evaluation plus nine re-evaluations over a thirty-four-month period.)

We first saw S when he was just three years old. At our initial evaluation, he understood ten to twenty-five words. He had six words of speech but he did not use them for communication. He walked clumsily and fell often. He was easily frustrated, and when he couldn't have his way, he had severe tantrums. He was extremely hyperactive and inattentive and unresponsive to all. His shirt was constantly wet from his incessant drooling.

Continuously he walked around seeking things he could bang together. His greatest pleasure was finding a metal wastepaper basket that he could turn over and then play like a drum. This had been a lifelong habit.

S's history revealed that he was an only child. There had been some spotting early in the pregnancy, so S's mother spent almost the entire first trimester of the pregnancy in bed. At birth S weighed 6½ pounds. The birth seemed routine, although the pediatrician reported that S was "sluggish" at birth, "probably due to the anesthesia." On the third day of life he developed a slight jaundice.

He was a quiet baby, crying only when hungry. His mother became increasingly concerned about his slow development, especially in speech, movement, and sociability. At age two he was a frightened, clumsy child who had no speech.

At twenty-six months of age he was evaluated at a university hospital. At that time he could not dress or feed himself. He had no speech except for an occasional "Da, da." He communicated by pointing and grunting.

The examination noted that he wandered aimlessly

around the room tapping objects in the room. He made no eye contact. One result of this examination was the raising of the question of whether this was infantile autism, because he seemed normal neurologically.

At this juncture, one professional informed S's mother that S was *autistic* and would, no doubt, *never talk*. Because S's mother would not accept this diagnosis and prognosis, she persisted in seeking help for her son. As a result, she was referred to another diagnostic facility. This facility agreed that S had problems of an emotional nature, and also added the label of mental retardation.

When S's persistent mother brought him, at age three, to us, I explained this theory of autism during the evaluation week. I asked her to observe him further, to evaluate his behavior, and to bring a report of his isms to the next re-evaluation.

Following our initial evaluation of S we programmed him as follows:

We had him follow a light in a darkened room. Also, we had his mother present him word cards with two-inch-high words printed on them.

We had his mother begin to control his sound environment. We placed his body in many different gravitational positions (for example, rolling, somersaults, upside down). Since we could not secure his cooperation for mobility, we "patterned" him. Three adults moved his body through the crawling and creeping motions to teach him the proprioception of movement. We also insisted that he spend a considerable amount of time on the floor, daily, to encourage his crawling and creeping, neither of which he did well.

He was towel rubbed and tactily stimulated. Tactility in general was prescribed. We also initiated dietary control.

The entire program took at least six hours per day of time.

In addition, his mother was to begin the activities at the survival stage. (Auditory)

At his second re-evaluation (after five months of home program), he was reading twenty words, was much calmer, and was saying a few more words. We added taste and smell activities to his program. We started an intensive auditory program aimed at ridding him of his constant tapping of objects (especially of metal scrap baskets). This program was based on his mother's observations of his auditory behavior. It included both whispering and the use of a stethoscope.

His mother reported that S's mannerisms continued, as did his tongue chewing. She reported that he was more observing. He had begun to read from a homemade book, but his writing was only scribbles. His drooling had decreased a bit. He called, "Mama" for the first time. His vocabulary was growing by leaps and bounds. He spoke in couplets. His understanding was much improved.

After eight months of program his mother reported at the third re-evaluation that he was now running and had learned to climb. Balance was better. He learned to ride his tricycle. He made attempts at dressing and undressing. Understanding was quite good. Now he spoke in sentences. His mannerisms were decreasing; his behavior was improved. He still scribbled, but his coloring had grown much better.

The drooling had stopped completely. Occasionally he had a tantrum, but he was happy and outgoing. When he saw children outdoors he joined right in with their activities.

At this time we cut down the amount of time he spent on the floor crawling and creeping and we cut the patterning in half. We added more practice with tastes and smell to his program. Also added was the recognition of numbers. We continued with reading exposure, along with the remainder of the program.

On his fourth re-evaluation, after eleven months of program, his drooling had stopped and never recurred. His speech was much improved. His behavior, although still not normal (especially in the auditory area), was much improved.

He was continued on a fairly intensive program of neurological organization, stressing auditory, visual, and much motor re-enforcement in the form of crawling and creeping. At this time he was allowed one day per week without any program to do.

At the fifth re-evaluation, after fifteen months of treatment, his mother reported that his speech had improved significantly. He conversed with people. He had some trouble mastering fine balance activities. He had shown a steady auditory improvement. His attention span was much improved, and his mannerisms had decreased. He had become vain about his clothing. His play had become more imaginative; he now talked to his toys. He had enjoyed playing with other children, but had not yet learned to take turns. His behavior had become much more manageable. At this re-evaluation we stopped the patterning and decreased the floor program. The visual, taste, smell, and auditory programs were continued. We asked S's mother to read a book on child management that stressed behavior modification. She felt that the book helped her to manage S better.

After seventeen months of treatment and at the time of his sixth re-evaluation, S had passed the entrance tests for nursery school. The evaluators were very pleased with his results on the test. He was borderline normal. His understanding was much improved, his coordination was much better. He spoke in eight- or nine-word sentences. He could cut with scissors. His reading was improving. His awareness was tremendously improved, and he seemed more mature.

On this visit we increased his auditory program, using primarily whispering when talking to him. The remainder of his program was kept essentially the same. Since he was doing well, we wanted him to have more time to spend with other children. We arranged to have him spend one-half hour per day outdoors with children.

His mother reported that he was able to understand more abstract concepts. His coordination continued to improve, as did his behavior. His mannerisms became rarer. He became more responsive to questions and asked more questions. His articulation had improved. Now he dressed and undressed himself. He had grown in independence and wanted to do more things for himself. His playmates tended to be slightly younger than he. His auditory awareness continued to improve. All was going well. His program remained essentially the same.

At his seventh re-evaluation, after twenty-three months of treatment, his mother reported that he was enjoying mornings in preschool. His hyperactivity was decreasing. Understanding continued to improve. He was still repeating a bit too much in speech. He enjoyed reading books that his mother made. He seemed less frustrated. Constantly he asked, "Is this right?" or "Is this funny?" At school he showed some aggressive behavior toward other children.

We encouraged his preschool placement and recommended practically no program other than to maintain an awareness of his sound environment. He was now ready to live in the sound environment of a group. Now that his mornings were spent at a preschool, our program was to be carried out informally, with continued work in whispering and on reading.

After twenty-seven months of treatment his mother told us that S had enjoyed this minimal program. He had learned to write a few letters. He was more sociable but was still too assertive with other children, though not as aggressive as he was. He had become less hyperactive.

After thirty months of treatment S's mother reported that he had learned to print a few words, but poorly. His auditory comprehension seemed perfect. His coordination was much improved, but he still had training wheels on his bike. He seemed more mature. His vocabulary had increased. He read longer sentences and had taught himself to spell. He had grown more cooperative, less childish, more independent, less hyperactive. His awareness was keen. He now got along well with his classmates.

S continued to make progress in speech, behavior, and learning during the next year of home treatment. We continued to see him and to change or modify his program at 4-month intervals. We started a laterality program with him after he had been on the program for 2½ years. We also began to occlude his left eye for a short period each day to create right-eyedness.

It has now been thirty-four months since S began the program. He was attending a normal kindergarten at the time of his last re-evaluation. He wrote spontaneously. He took care of all his personal needs, including dressing himself. He was completing a first grade mathematics workbook, and enjoyed doing the work. His auditory comprehension was excellent, and his spoken vocabulary was normal for his age group. He enjoyed reading first grade books and spelling games.

He has a friendly personality, gets along well with his

classmates, is independent and self-confident. He is keenly aware of everything and everyone around him.

He has made a total of ten visits during the two years and ten months of treatment and is now on long-range observation.

At the three-year anniversary of his beginning treatment, his mother reported by mail as follows:

> S is progressing well in the second Sullivan reader and is able to read books of the difficulty of *Green Eggs and Ham.* He is three-fourths of the way through the Addison-Wesley Arithmetic 1 with adequate understanding of most areas. The greatest over-all improvement he has made since October is in the area of self-control and self-discipline. His outbursts of anger and frustration are less frequent and are better handled. He is more receptive to reason and control. His general coordination is better and he has improved in handling a ball and in other physical skills. He still needs some help and encouragement in dressing and undressing himself and in bathing himself, but all of this shows gradual improvement.

CASE P.

(Evaluation, one week, plus sixteen one-day re-evaluations over a four-year period.)

This was a difficult pregnancy. There was early spotting, and P's mother spent most of the first seven months of the pregnancy in bed. There was constant threat of miscarriage until the seventh month. Then all seemed normal, for the last two months.

Although P developed reasonably normally, he didn't "act like other children." He had "behavior mannerisms," his parents reported. P gagged and vomited when switched from strained to junior foods, and again, when changed to solids. At seven months he sat alone. At thirteen months he walked. He started to talk at two and a half years, but to stuffed animals—very seldom to people. Until age six, his speech consisted of his repeating words he heard.

When we first saw him, P's problems were: coordination; lack of comprehension; speech reversals; immaturity; irritability; and behavior mannerisms. His attention was always on trivia. These behaviors and subjects at this time were: flying saucers; snow tires; sounds with tongue; giggling inappropriately; and holding things in front of his eyes. He banged objects constantly, hit his chin, and constantly made facial grimaces. He held his hands on his head and he rocked. Also, he picked at his lips. All these behaviors occurred constantly.

His parents had taken P to many specialists in child development. Among his diagnoses were: 1. autism; 2. personality disorder; 3. mental retardation; and 4. childhood schizophrenia.

Kindergarten had been a disaster for P. Because of the problems, he was referred for many examinations. As a result, he was sent for psychiatric treatment and to a speech class.

Tests indicated he would be completely unable to cope with first grade academically, and that his disruptive behavior without provocation might endanger the other children. I.Q. tests were consistently low.

During our initial evaluation, it was obvious that P had sensoryisms in smell (he smelled everything in sight); in vision (he constantly rocked and waved his hands in front of his eyes); and in hearing (he made sounds, or constantly, repetitively spoke words to himself that he had "heard").

In order to help P through the survival stage, we took him out of school, where he was doing poorly. We gave him a home program aimed at smell, audition, and vision, in addition to a complete program of neurological organization.

By the end of the first year, his smellisms had disappeared, but his visual and auditory isms continued, although somewhat diminished. He also continued to giggle inappropriately. His understanding was improved and he was speaking more, although he still spent most of his time talking to himself.

We continued a central program and a survival program, even though most of his isms had decreased significantly. We also had him return to school for two hours a day.

By the end of the second year of treatment, his sensoryisms were almost all gone. His reading was at a high second grade level and his writing had improved. His speech had improved significantly.

He was still somewhat vague in his interactions with others. We continued a fairly heavy program. Since his behavior was much improved, we allowed him to be in school for four hours a day. He spent the remainder of the day doing our program.

After three years, his sensoryisms were gone. He conversed with others willingly, but other children often took advantage of him. He was not able to be self-assertive.

His reading was much improved, as were his writing and spelling. We placed him in school for a full day. The school agreed to help him to begin to join some social activities of the regular class.

We last saw P at the end of his fourth year of treatment. His I.Q. fell within the normal range. He scored within the eighth grade level in oral reading, but his test scores on standardized tests given in a group situation were still very low.

He is attending a special class and is in process of attending a few classes, daily, with the regular sixth grade.

His writing remains his weakest school subject. He is taking one academic subject with the regular sixth grade class, plus art, gym, and shop. As he improves, he will be transitioned into more classes with this normal sixth grade group.

He gets along well with the other children when playing handball, or swimming, or attending boxing class. He is still in need of improvement when in free social situations with the normal group.

CASE A.

(Evaluation, one week, plus nine one-day visits over a twenty-five-month period.)

We first saw A when he was three years and ten months old. He had been diagnosed as: 1. autistic; 2. aphasic; 3. deaf; and 4. mentally retarded, by specialists who had seen him up to this time.

He had been born of a pregnancy marred by some mild spotting during the second trimester. He was an extremely quiet baby. He did not walk until he was twenty months old.

When we first saw him, he had ten to twenty-five words of speech and he seemed to understand about the same number of words. He was very easily upset because of his inability to express himself. He paid attention to sounds and speech only when he wanted to. On occasion, he seemed deaf. He generally ignored commands or requests. He seemed lost in his own little world.

He made many noises of his own but rarely paid attention to sounds coming from others. He had been through many evaluations, especially auditory evaluations. He had also received speech stimulation therapy.

Following our initial evaluation, we placed him on an auditory survival program of loud sound effects plugged into his ears through inserted earpieces; tape recordings of his family, turned loud; noise makers; shouting; loud talk; and laughing. In addition, we placed him on a maximal program of neurological organization. We also instituted a visual stimulation program.

At his second visit we deleted visual training from his program and increased the auditory program. In addition to the former auditory activities, he was now given loud, single words via a tape recorder for as much as two hours per day. At the same time, we started to introduce the same words visually, on large-size flash cards.

At his third visit, his coordination was improved. He was saying small sentences but only when he wanted something very much. Otherwise he preferred to use a single word. His noise-making had decreased and he seemed a bit more "tuned in." He could now follow a two-step verbal command, but with great effort. We added stethoscope use and whispering to his program.

On his fourth visit, his auditory intake was increasing. His vocabulary was increasing; he was using four- to six-word sentences. He was less "tuned out," and more interested in sounds and speech. He was learning to write words.

On his fifth visit, he was reversing in his writing. We were working on establishing complete right-sidedness. He was attending preschool for three hours per day and was becoming more involved with the other children. Hearing was still his main problem; so we decided to try hearing aids to see if we could break through in this area.

On his sixth visit, we decided that his reading and writing activities were quite advanced for a preschooler; hence, we eased up on this aspect of the program. We continued to work on developing complete right-sidedness and to work on his auditory intake. We asked his parents to arrange for placement tests for kindergarten.

At the seventh visit he was doing so well in auditory intake that we decreased the program to include balance activities, hearing inputs, and kindergarten attendance.

At his next visit, the eighth, we continued an even milder and less formal program. His speech continued to improve as did his relationships with those around him. He had "joined our world."

At our last visit, we suggested that he continue to use the stethoscope and whispering alternately, and we continued to encourage his use of tape recorder and walkie-talkie.

One year later, his parents reported that he was in a learning disability class for children with auditory problems. He takes some classes with normal children. The parents wrote: "Your protege is blossoming every day." He has a rapidly expanding vocabulary, with twelve or more 1-word sentences, and good sentence structure. Articulation, though, is still poor. His verbal comprehension is also improving, and A doesn't depend as much on visual aids as previously. His coordination and writing are much improved. He reads well and his visual memory is excellent. He is starting to learn phonics. He is a good-natured, friendly boy whose social adjustments, although sometimes painful if with peers without problems, are improving.

CASE T.
(Age 9. Cooperative evaluation for survival.)

T's case is a failure. Although we had been treating T for years, we had not changed his behavior. He exhibited sensoryisms in many areas. Such children are extremely difficult to diagnose. Since we were making no progress and since we were faced with such a complex problem of diagnosis, we decided to ask for help in diagnosis and in treatment ideas from his parents and from those who worked with him at home.

T had been labeled autistic by many specialists. His parents had been constantly urged to institutionalize him, but they resisted. He lives at home with his mother, father, and five siblings. He is taught five hours per week by a homebound teacher, trained in special education. He is also taught one hour per week, on a volunteer basis, by a teacher who regularly teaches a normal second grade class.

In my effort to gather help in making a diagnosis of T, I gave a copy of the manuscript of this book to each of the following:

1. His mother.
2. His father, whom I had never oriented.
3. His homebound teacher, whom I had met once.
4. His volunteer teacher, whom I had never met.

I asked each of them to read the manuscript and to submit an independent report on their observations of T's behavior.

This is the report prepared by T's mother:

Tactility

Body is warm. Likes to stroke self gently with quilt. Great increase in belly tickling recently. When I tickle his face he takes my hands for more. Puts tongue on things. Lies on stomach and moves around gently (a kind of masturbation).

Bites right wrist and left palm. Sits with both legs back and thumps on rear. Bangs back of head and/or back against walls and couches. Rocks a lot in car, whether or not the car is in motion. Bangs right side of head with fist.

Has seemingly meaningless outbursts. Flaps cords, socks, ribbons, strings, etc., against right side of face past ear and eye. Sometimes shivers, for no reason.

Auditory

Light sleeper. Can't stand things in ears. Dogs, haircuts, brass instruments, whistles, and hammering frighten him.

Makes lots of loud noises, laughs, shrieks. Gets very close to TV speaker and to vacuum cleaner. Didn't mind organ in stairwell, when right under it, though the mother's head almost popped. Tears paper. Lately a big increase in teeth grinding.

Rocking and odd positions. Preoccupation with sounds. Always holds his left hand behind his left ear whenever he has a spoon in his right hand.

Smell

Membranes of nose easily irritated by cold. He rubs and rubs it. When really allergic whole sinus area across cheeks and nose get very red.

Rapid nose breathing, especially if stuffy. Does hand blowing, especially when eating and in some new place. He blows air into his cupped hand and guides it toward his nose.

Vision

Moves head from side to side but in downward motion to shoulder. Rocks a lot—sitting regularly in a chair, on knees with palms on floor, on haunches with hands palm down behind. Often noisy while he is rocking. Occasional finger play. Pupils sometimes dilated. Seems to look through people and things.

Taste

Puts tongue on many things.

Only likes scrapple, hamburgers, or hot dogs that are somewhat spicy.

Lots of tongue chewing.

Doesn't mind salt, sugar, or pickle juice or anything else but vanilla. (That could be smell.)

He has a high palate.

He has a constant, unquenchable thirst.

This is the report of his father:

Tactility

Does not resist being touched. Is not bothered by touch of clothing. Is not bothered by temperature variations. He has taken warm and cold baths with no variation in behavior. Body is not tense to touch. He *does* gently tickle himself.

He *bites* himself.

Does repetitive body activities.

He likes to bounce his back, and back of head, while sitting on a couch.

Will shiver as though some unseen object has touched him.

He is subject to "tactile outbursts."

The tickling, referred to previously, could be scratching nonexistent bites.

T seems to fit the "white noise" tactile category.

Smell

T does not exhibit any behaviors that would indicate a problem.

Auditory

He is bothered by loud noises. Many times his face is ashen.

Many times he will move toward sound. That is, he loves the noise of the vacuum cleaner. Many times he will place his ear close to the TV set.

He detests haircuts.

Rainstorms do not seem to trouble him.

He loves to take baths, hot or cold.

The surf does not seem to bother him.

He likes being in the bathroom.

He likes the vacuum cleaner.

He likes to tear paper.

He likes toys with moving parts.

He likes to rock his head.

Taste

He is a picky eater.

He will drink anything.

Vision

Likes to rock.

Likes to move objects in front of his face, such as a belt or tie.

Not afraid of the dark or of heights.

This is the report of T's homebound teacher, who had had special education training:

Tactility

Sensitive hands. Doesn't like to be held or touched a lot.

Feels ribs with tips of fingers.

Fingers are hot.

Bites hands when angry.
Hits head again and again.
Nose bothers him when upset.
Chews tongue.

Smell

Pushes people away.
Blows air from mouth to nose.
Becomes tense when he has a cold.
Moves away from me during menstruation.

Auditory

Noises cause mood changes.
Problem sleeping.
Dislikes haircuts, sirens.
Loves to look at rain.
Leaves a room suddenly.
Rocks.
Does hang in weird positions in bed.

Taste

Picky about food (except liquids and sweets), but pretty
normal, on the whole.

Vision

Does stare.
Visual recall is good.
Rocking.
Waves tie and hand in front of face.

This is the report of the volunteer teacher, who teaches
a normal class of second-graders. I had never met this
teacher. She saw T once a week.

Tactility

Wrist biting accompanied by crying and shouting. He bites the right wrist. The outbursts seem to last anywhere from fifteen seconds to two or three minutes. Recently I was able to stop him by simply repeatedly taking his arm out of his mouth. At other times he has bitten his wrist when his allergies have bothered him or he has a cold.

Banging his chest against the table while sitting next to me, sometimes including banging his back against the chair, usually accompanied by sounds. I usually interpret this as his attempts to "work up" to saying something to me by practicing, and finally blending, sounds into a word or a few words. Often when I ask him if he knows a certain word, he taps the "Y" Scrabble piece to signify "Yes." He does this every second or third visit. Some days he's quite content not to communicate through verbal sounds but by spelling out his ideas with Scrabble letters.

Sucks tongue. Fans with hand just below his face.

Used to touch area just behind his ear.

Licked different things—nubby material, table.

Put things in mouth—pieces of games.

Rocks back and forth while sitting on legs on floor.

Places tongue between teeth a good part of the time, while I'm working with him.

Used to "lick" (feel with his tongue, not stroke) different-textured objects; for example, nubby fabric on couch, tabletop, small pieces of games. (He'd put them in his mouth.)

Rocks back and forth while sitting on legs (every other visit).

Fans with hand just below face—occasionally now, more frequently six months ago.

Smell

Places hand over mouth and nose and blows air from mouth.

He does cry, scream and rub his nose when he has a cold or his allergies are bothering him.

Hearing

Clicking of tongue inside mouth (or clicking of throat); used to be constant, now more rare.

Smacking of tongue between lips; used to be frequent, now rare.

Palpates objects we're using in instruction (Cuisinaire rods, coins, Scrabble pieces). Drops them from varying heights, one inch, eight to ten inches, or three feet or so. Also taps the objects rhythmically. All this is occasional now; used to be constant six months ago.

Bangs hand against head while shouting, only once in a while now.

Shouts while rocking, every second or third visit now; used to be every visit.

Used to put finger behind left ear; doesn't do this any more.

Crinkles or tears paper—occasionally.

Likes (or used to, 1½ years ago) a noisy bell-ringing toy lawn mower and visually "popping" toy.

Screaming outbursts 2 out of every 3 visits.

Holding string, rope, or cord, etc., in 2 hands between chest and ear and vibrating it rhythmically—occasional now; used to be every visit.

Taste

Sucks his own tongue—every visit.

Vision

Rocks back and forth, sometimes while making sounds, sometimes silently—every other visit.

Stares through people—used to be constant, now only 50 percent to 75 percent of time I'm visiting. Though he appears (I think as a psychological game) *not* to be focusing on the objects of the material game we're using, he does pick out the object that is appropriate—90 percent to 95 percent of the time. He makes eye contact and smiles (at the same time) at me every time I visit now, at least once per visit.

At a conference following the submission of these reports, it was decided that T obviously had problems in tactility and in vision. During the discussion, it soon became apparent that one very disturbing sensory area for T was the area of hypersmell. As a result of the *cooperative* effort, a working plan could be made for T's survival. We cooperatively decided to start treating the smell, tactility, and vision at the survival level. He continues on the program as outlined, but is only making minimal progress.

CASE M.

(One-week evaluation and twenty-three one-day re-evaluations over a five-year, four-month period.)

M first came for evaluation when he was a ten-and-a-half-year-old boy. M had one brother who was five years older. M's mother had had one miscarriage prior to his conception and two more subsequently.

Throughout the pregnancy his mother was afflicted with extreme nausea and dizziness. Until the seventh month of her pregnancy with M the doctor could hear no heart sounds and there was little fetal movement. There was false labor one week prior to his birth, and his mother was hospitalized for two days. When M was finally born, labor was induced and was very quick—two and a half hours.

At first M's parents considered him a normal baby, although he had some trouble sucking from a bottle. However, when he was fifteen months old, they began to worry; he was still neither walking nor talking. At eighteen months M had German measles with a high fever. When he was three years old M's parents took him to a hospital for several days of testing. The results were a diagnosis of brain damage. One year later another neurological examination confirmed this diagnosis. Meanwhile, M was becoming hyperactive. Another doctor prescribed Dilantin "to calm him down." After trying Dilantin for one year M's mother saw no change in him and stopped it.

It should be noted that when M was five and a half he had been enrolled in a kindergarten, where he remained until he was seven and a half; but he just couldn't keep up with the other children. He was then enrolled in a special class. He was given psychological testing by the local board of education and was diagnosed as "emotionally disturbed." He was again tested a year later, by the school psychologist. This time he was diagnosed as "schizophrenic autistic."

When M was brought to us for evaluation, he was physically healthy, but had many disturbing characteristics. He had a very short attention span and was quite hyperactive. He squinted his eyes and had a peering look. (This in spite of the fact that he had had a recent, thorough visual eye examination and had been prescribed glasses.) He had a peculiar characteristic of repeating everything that was said to him. He bit his fingers and constantly touched his face, concentrating on his eyes, nose, and mouth. He loved to play with string in a meaningless way. He would pretend that his arm was a crane and keep it up for hours. He daily spent hours talking to himself. Above all, he had many "smellisms." He would smell everything, but particularly his own fingers. He would touch objects or people and then smell his fingers.

At his first evaluation it was found that he could not use one leg in a skilled role, such as hopping. He walked and ran uncoordinately. His crawling and creeping were extremely poor. The production of speech was rated as poor. It was found that he had very immature manual abilities.

He had poor near point convergence of vision, with an alternating divergent strabismus when looking at an object held close to his nose. His auditory understanding was that of a five-year-old. He could read a few words.

His parents were given a program to be carried out at home. Essentially, the program consisted of patterning, crawling and creeping, auditory stimulation, visual exercises, masking, and smell practice.

Because of his strange repetitive behaviors, especially playing with string, smelling his fingers, and the constant repetition of anything said to him, M was rejected by almost everybody except his parents.

We carefully oriented his parents relative to his sensory problems (smell, vision, and tactility), and we asked them to supplement our program with as much practice as possible in these areas.

M's parents spent hours daily working with his smell, vision, and tactility, in addition to following our prescribed program.

M was re-evaluated at approximately three-month intervals. After a year on the program M was speaking in longer sentences and the content was more appropriate to his age. He was reading first grade workbooks independently and could copy sentences both in cursive and printing. He was succeeding with arithmetic and was learning the multiplication tables. He had become more self-assertive and could cross streets by himself and go shopping for his mother. He was now eager to try things that a normal boy would do at the amusement park or on the beach. The staff was delighted with him.

M continued to be reassessed at three-month intervals. By the end of his second year of treatment he had shown much progress. In the intervening year we decided to establish complete right-sidedness. He could now write spontaneous sentences. He could now take a standard reading test independently, scoring 2.6 in vocabulary and 2.2 in comprehension. His walking, running, and general coordination were much better than ever before. He now played with children closer to his own age and could compete with them. Above all, he was developing a sense of humor. His program was adjusted for full reinforcement of right-sidedness.

At the end of the third year M had advanced so much that he was administered a battery of standard achievement tests, including the Stanford Achievement Test, the Gray Oral Reading Test, and the Ammons and Ammons Quick Test. He scored so well that he was given third and fourth grade reading workbooks to do at home. It was noted that his writing continued to improve, as did his speech and auditory comprehension. The parents reported that he was more independent and outgoing; in fact, he was becoming downright aggressive! His program was adjusted to place more stress on academics, to reinforce his schoolwork. He was told that on future visits for re-evaluation he must wear a coat and tie. (He was now nearly fourteen, an age at which appearances are important.)

At the end of the fourth year, now nearly fifteen years

old, and in an ungraded class at school, M was becoming an inveterate reader. His parents reported that "he reads anything." The isms were nearly gone, and he could maintain himself very well during a two-hour battery of academic testing. There was a vast improvement in him visually. His eyes now moved smoothly in their orbits, his eye-hand coordination was much better, and convergence was nearly perfect.

Nearly a year later M was promoted to a reading test appropriate to the fifth and sixth grades, because he could now successfully identify words at the fifth grade level. His visual acuity for distance had improved so much that he now wore glasses only for reading. During the summer he had gone almost daily to a neighborhood youth center by himself. He was now getting better at throwing and catching, could swim, and ride a bike. Most impressive of all, his I.Q. had increased nearly twenty points over the preceding year.

CASE H.

(One-week evaluation plus five one-day re-
evaluations over a fourteen-month period.)

H's birth was three weeks overdue. His mother was unduly fatigued; hence the obstetrician decided to induce labor with medication. He was born precipitously (under two hours of labor). There were no complications. Although no statement was made relative to H's condition, he seemed perfectly normal to his mother, who saw him immediately. There was no delay in birth cry; he seemed normal in every way. He presented no problems as an infant. His early months were exactly what his siblings' early months of development were.

By the time H was eighteen months old his mother had

become quite concerned about him because his speech consisted only of his repeating what was said to him. He could not communicate. His behavior became increasingly strange, filled with many repetitive activities, such as constantly waving his hands in front of his face, making strange sounds, and acting out of contact with others—indeed, ignoring people around him.

At age three H was taken to the hospital for three days of tests because of his strange behavior and lack of speech. The diagnosis was "emotionally disturbed," with a very poor prognosis. There was no recommended therapy other than institutionalization.

H attended "special" nursery schools from age four through seven, with no change in his symptoms. At age seven he was attending a psychiatric institute. Because of lack of change, he was again placed in "special class" in the public schools. During these years he had numerous tests of a psychological nature. His mother was never given the actual reports, but in conferences she was given a number of "tentative" diagnoses. The most consistent were: autism and schizophrenia, with a negative prognosis.

H was first seen at the Institutes when he was eight years old. He was a handsome boy who walked on his toes, spending his time playing with his fingers, waving his hands before his eyes, and periodically making noises or laughing out of context. If talked to, he would ignore the communication and, if forced to pay attention, would only repeat what had been said to him. He seemed to be in a world of his own and resisted and resented any intrusion into his world. He was not a problem of management if left alone to play with his fingers or wave his hands. But if an examiner persisted, H would react by having a violent temper tantrum and crying.

Functional evaluations on his first visit were as follows: His mobility was that of a seven-year-old. His language function, when he cooperated, was that of a five-year-old, but he rarely functioned at that level. His hand use was approximately that of a seven-year-old. He could understand verbal commands at the five-year-old level, when forced by his mother to cooperate. In tactile competence he operated as a six-year-old. He could speak hundreds of words and sentences at approximately a five-year-old level, but rarely in his life chose to do so. Interestingly enough, he read at a first grade level at the beginning of the program, although he constantly lost his place in reading, or he chose to do something else.

When, on his first visit to the Institutes, he was forced by his mother or evaluators to cooperate, his over-all functioning placed him at a low five-year-old level. His handwriting was large and almost illegible. He was hypotactile.

It was our opinion that his aberrant behavior was symptomatic of his many perceptual problems. For example, he played constantly with his fingers to improve his poor tactility. He waved his hands in front of his eyes in an attempt to improve his visual function. He shouted periodically, due to his inability to deal with the faulty auditory perceptions arriving at his brain. We theorized that if the perceptual abilities could be improved these behaviors and aberrant functions would disappear.

The treatment prescribed was auditory and visual stimulation, based on the premise that stimulation given in logical developmental order with increased frequency, intensity, and duration would develop more acceptable perceptual abilities. If accomplished, sensory inputs would no longer be considered intrusions by H and his behavior might be changed. H carried out the program of sensory stimulation at home with his mother. He resisted at the outset, but adjusted to the routine rather well.

He was re-evaluated three months later. His mother reported that he was more alert and more "tuned in," enjoyed the reading and arithmetic assignments, and seemed, to her, to be speaking more.

During this interval he was again seen by his psychiatrist, who once again strongly recommended *institutionalization*. Our re-evaluation indicated that H had made no improvement on the functional profile, but we did see some slight improvement in his awareness. The program was revised slightly, with the addition of more and varied *auditory* stimulation.

Two months later H was re-evaluated again. His coordination had improved, especially his walking. Now he occasionally responded with speech. Both his writing and reading had improved. He was calmer and slightly more attentive to the world around him. He would now answer questions with a "yes" or "no," and he was "turning off" the world much less. He seemed much more responsive. The physical aspects of the program were increased and the sensory stimulation was kept constant. For the next re-evaluation the objective to achieve was no more "turning off" the world.

Four months later H was seen again. He had gained two months in functional evaluation and, remarkably, he no longer "turned off" the world! His coordination was much improved. He had learned to ride a bike. His writing and reading were much improved (second grade level), and his conversation was better. His vocabulary was also significantly improved. H was studying geography and was doing well at arithmetic.

His mother reported that he was calmer, friendlier, liked people, was more inquisitive, less shy, noticed more things, now watched TV and, for the first time, went near other children when playing.

The most significant change was that he no longer made odd sounds and rarely waved fingers and hands in front of his eyes. We continued with the basic program. In light of his excellent progress, we deleted some of the visual aspects of the program.

H returned in four months. There was no change in his functional evaluation. There was a negative change, in that once again he waved his hands in front of his eyes. We had erred in deleting the visual aspects of his program too soon. They were now reinstated and increased.

At the last re-evaluation his reading was excellent—at grade level. He enjoyed geography, wrote well, and rarely "turned off." Instead, he was now quite "tuned in" to everything around him. He was constantly searching and talking, interrupting and asking, to the point of being considered hyperactive. He related to the staff and became stubborn about doing the home program. He called me a "stupid idiot" because he was angry with one aspect of the program. He listened carefully to anything that involved him. He no longer cried unless truly angry. He argued with the staff over the program. He no longer "turned off" except on rare lapses into the finger waving in front of his eyes.

As of that moment in his treatment H's coordination, his learning ability, and his academic performance were almost normal. His speech was excellent when he cooperated. His level on our functional evaluation indicated that his mobility, manual competence, visual ability (reading), and tactile competence were quite good. His weaker areas were understanding spoken language and speech, both of which had improved significantly as his attention span improved. His remaining perceptual problems were primarily auditory and, secondarily, visual and tactile. He could now be dealt with as a hyperactive and mildly uncooperative child.

At this point H had completed the survival stage and was ready now to move into the central treatment stage.

CASE B.
(One-week evaluation plus eighteen one-day re-evaluations over a four-year, eleven-month period.)

B was sent to us by a neurologist who was one of many specialists who had seen her. B was a middle child, born of an uneventful pregnancy and birth. The first eight months of life were spent almost entirely in crying. One of her eyes was crossed.

From the age of two to seventeen months she suffered many "blackouts." She cried out and then could not take her next breath. Her mother gave her mouth-to-mouth resuscitation on many occasions. Hunger and fatigue seemed to be the precipitating factors in these episodes.

The following are B's mother's notes on her early development:

7 days—Colic begins, lasting 8 months (the first 4 months steady and intense). During these first 4 months regular night sleep pattern—12 midnight to 6 A.M.—crying steadily all remaining hours, except for 2-hour sleep time in 10-minute naps. Crying began to diminish at 4 months; gone by 5 months.

3 weeks—Umbilical hernia. Rx tape.

1 month—Will smile and respond to singing and rocking.

2 months—Holds head up. Looks around when lying on stomach. Smiles at objects.

4 months—X-ray hip for congenital dislocation. Negative. Watch eye crossing.

4½ months—Deliberately reaches for and grasps things tightly. Sits in jumper seat 1–1½ hours.

5 months—Reaches for things with both hands. Plays with toes.

7 months—Throws toys on floor and looks to see where they fell. Eyes (crossing) improving. Articulating small amount. Responds with laughter to other children, enjoys watching them. Has always slept on stomach. Uses pacifier.

7½ months—Turns completely over, from back to stomach.

8 months—Sits in feeding table. Sits well by self but unable to get self into sitting position. Rocks hard in jumper seat and beginning to stand with this support. Says "ga ga" and "da da." Brother is very rough and often hits her on head (not hard). She loves his attention, excited. Enjoys looking at pictures. No teeth.

9 months—Enjoys tearing magazine pages.

10 months—Crawls backward. Eyes bothering her. Shakes head back and forth. Sometimes squints up eyes. Has 2 teeth.

First accident—fell out of stroller, which rolled down incline. Fell on face on concrete. Scratched.

Puts only fingers into mouth.

11 months—Stands without support. Kneels and rolls over. Can now pull self to sitting position and sit. Makes all syllable noises.

12 months—Pulls self to standing position in playpen. Will stand holding on for 1 minute on toes. Has never yet worn shoes. Started to crawl forward. Right eye still turns in occasionally. Likes to hold onto and carry around her plastic underpants.

13 months—Says "didi" and waves goodbye.

15 months—Walks holding onto person or furniture. Loves to be cuddled. Hugs dolls and stuffed animals.

16 months—Stands alone and walks alone on flat feet (since wearing shoes). Still on bottle. Does not drink well from cup. Says "Buce, Mamom, Da Da Da."

16½ months—Climbs into child-size rocking chair and rocks self. Climbs up stairs and up onto furniture. Into everything, always under foot.

Up until now (16½ months) B has "fainted" about 40 times since she was 2 months old. This is beginning to decrease in frequency but increase in severity (severity being measured by duration of period of unconsciousness and difficulty to revive, i.e., mouth-to-mouth resuscitation required). Longest period probably under ½ minute. These episodes have initiated with one long, hard cry, with the expulsion of all the air and then the prolonged delay in taking the next breath, during which time color is ashen, lips blue, eyes roll back, body limp, no muscular spasms evident. Peak of frequency 14–16 months. Beginning to decrease at 16½ months. Hunger and/or tiredness present on days when she was relaxed.

17 months—Begins to occasionally sleep on back. Points to things.

19 months—Smells everything, instead of exploring with mouth and hands. Throws everything.

2 years—Has not fainted in 6 months. Wants pacifier most of the time.

2½ years—Repeats everything (short phrases). Uses pacifier during waking hours. Compulsions—must have shoes tied quickly and sleeves pushed above elbows.

2¾ years—Occasionally does not nap. Climbs out of crib. Puts 2–3 words together. 1–2 bottles a day.

3½ years—Short phrases. Moved. Sister was born when B was 2½ years old. B was toilet trained at this time and easily, by grandmother. Terrified if mother is out of sight. Much concentration of attention on her clothing. Starts nursery school.

3¾ years—Tensional outlets—rapid, repetitious questions and incessant chatter. Scratching and pinching substitutes for hitting.

B attended a small nursery school for ages 3 through 5. Because of her strange behavior she was not accepted into first grade, but was placed in a special class. B's parents were extremely concerned with her strange behavior. They sought help from many sources. These are the diagnoses and treatments that she received, again from B's mother's notes:

History of Diagnosis and Treatment

Age 4 years—Medical center. Dx: Autism. Made by psychologist. Rx: Referred to local children's psychiatric center for long-term follow-up program. Prognosis: dismal, nearly hopeless.

Age 5 years—Children's psychiatric center. Dx: Severe emotional disturbance; not autistic. Made through one week's observation and evaluation in small controlled nursery school for disturbed children. Rx: Recommended enrollment in their nursery school.

Age 5—Evaluation at a Neurological Institute. Dx: Minimal, diffuse brain damage, made on bases of neurological examination, skull plates, PKU and EEG.

1. Visual perceptual deficit.
2. Weak motor coordination.
3. Some emotional problem overlaying these.

Rx: Referred to psychologist for determination of intellectual potential.

Age 5—Psychologist. Dx: A "different" child. Not to be classified as mentally retarded, although 8–9 months behind intellectually. No evidence of emotional problem. Slight coordination deficit. Felt that B should have been allowed to enter kindergarten. Rx: A good nursery school for remainder of school year, thus initiating her third complete year of nursery school, each one a different school.

We first saw B when she was eight years and three months old. She did not like to be touched, and she did not choose to touch anything. She explored everything and everyone by smelling them. She asked constant, repetitive questions.

What characterized her most was her fear and her repetitiveness. She had great fear of people touching her and felt threatened by doctors, whom she felt would "operate on me." She became upset whenever her parents left her sight. She talked constantly, repeating the same questions for hours on end.

She always walked on tiptoes and seemed to bounce on them as she walked. Her walk was quite uncoordinated.

Our survival program was as follows:

Patterning. This required three people to move her body through a crawling motion. The problem was that she was hypertactile and, at the outset, was very upset by people touching her body and moving her through the patterning motions. We had her spend much time on the floor in crawling, hoping to smooth out her crawling motion.

A full program aimed at decreasing her hypertactility was initiated. This included towel rubs, placing special emphasis on tactility with her hands and forearms. An auditory program was instituted. We both magnified and suppressed sound, since we were not yet sure whether she was hyper- or hypoauditory. We also initiated a visual program for a child who is hypo in vision. Since she was neither succeeding nor surviving in school, we withdrew her from school. We began to work on her smellisms.

By the end of the first year of treatment (three one-day visits) her smell behavior had reduced significantly, but it was still present. Her crawling, creeping, and walking were much more coordinated. She was calmer and was able to touch many more things with her hands without first smelling them. She could write three words and, most significantly, she now permitted us to touch her. She seemed more mature and cooperative. As a result, we requested a homebound tutor for B. We continued our program, adding greater stress on tactility and vision. In addition, we began to establish complete right-sidedness.

At the end of two years of treatment B was touching or looking and only rarely smelling. She no longer pinched her siblings. Her hand use had improved but was still poor. She had completed first grade reading. Her speech was much better. She was much more cooperative, but still balked at difficult tasks. She repeated only occasionally. She would stop repeating, if reprimanded. She reported an occasional dizzy spell, which was of short duration. She continued to have strange sensations in her eyes. She had changed so much that we decided to send her to school. She was placed in a normal second grade group on a trial basis. In a few months she was moved out of the normal class into a nongraded class. She could not complete the independent assignments given in the regular class.

During the third year of treatment B's smellisms totally disappeared. She had learned to stop her occasional dizzy spells by "squeezing her eyelids shut." She became more cooperative and less fearful when tested. She scored in the third grade in reading. She seemed so much more mature that she was placed in a regular fourth grade class. For one hour each day B left the regular class for special help in writing. She received new glasses because of increasing nearsightedness. She was trying harder to complete her work independently. Her fourth grade teacher reported that B still teased other children and was not attentive enough to group instruction. We continued to work on her tactility, vision, and auditory capacities. In addition, we continued to work toward complete right-sidedness.

At the end of four years and eleven months of treatment

(a total of eighteen one-day re-evaluation visits), B was surviving in a normal fifth grade classroom. Her reading was at a sixth grade level, when she was tested alone. She still had trouble taking group tests. She was more mature, had stopped repeating questions, and no longer smelled things. She tolerated being touched and she had written her first short story. She had had no dizzy spells for a year. She scored at low normal on an I.Q. test. She was no longer fearful with strangers or with other children.

At that time B made an early sixth grade level test score on an individual oral reading and comprehension test. Taking standardized group tests still presented a problem to B. Her teacher reported that she was a tease in class and still had trouble getting down to her work. Her handwriting remained poor. She was generally calmer at home than at school. Emotional outbursts were not as intense and were of shorter duration.

Her parents reported at this final visit, "She has been accepted as a normal student in a small private school and will stay in a normal class."

EPILOGUE

I embarked on this journey into the world of the autistic child reluctantly and fearfully. The children whom I met at the outset were strangers; I dubbed them "the ultimate strangers." Our first real contacts were not through words. Those first contacts were fleeting glances, then frightened exploratory touches, building up to tenuous embraces, to honest and meaningful tears—and finally to words. Those brave children who made the frightening journey from their world into our world seemed to be growing through a new kind of growth process, whose birth cry was a fleeting glance of recognition that happily blossomed into trust and friendship. Only after that birth cry could we begin to teach each other about our very different worlds.

As I learned about their world I could look at these children through new eyes. I told their parents what I saw. Parents learn quickly. To see parents and their formerly alien children finally look into each other's eyes and talk to each other made my trip worthwhile. As the parents understood, they and their children were no longer strangers living under the same roof but in alien worlds. As the children learned to look beyond things toward people, as they began to hear beyond their own strange sounds toward the sounds of human voices, as they became able to tolerate our strange touches, smells, and tastes, they began to recognize those of us around them as people. As the children began to see and hear people, the sadness was lifted from the eyes of their parents. As this happened, hope could be seen growing in the faces of their parents. Hope has not been a very popular word in this field, but the first spontaneous contact made by a parent and child was always productive of hope. I quickly found that after that first parent-child contact was made, no matter how brief or fleeting, an increase in the speed of progress followed.

These children taught me that they were misunderstood. They taught me that they were even incorrectly named. They are not psychotic, they are brain-injured. They are not seeking abandonment through their alien and seemingly rejective behavior; instead they are desperately trying to free themselves from their inner prisons, prisons whose bars are created by sensory distortions. I learned that their strange behavior is a frightened last-ditch attempt to survive—and I learned that the survival stage is where most of the failure took place. I also learned that there were other types of children, given different names by different professional groups, who were in reality the same children with different names. Their problems were the same. They also lived in a sensory distorted world, they also had strange behavioral mannerisms, they also needed help. As a result I began to see not only those children diagnosed as autistic by some outside professional but also those children who were given different labels but exhibited the same behavior as the autistic children.

There were children with whom I failed—even to elicit

that first glance of recognition or that first communicating touch. We remained strangers to each other. For them we have not learned enough, for them we must learn more. I agree with the others in the field that statistics and controlled studies are meaningless in an area where failure is the general rule. We are still in the early stage of search instead of at the research stage of knowledge. Each child helped to survive, each child integrated into our world brings us a milestone closer to the solution of the problem of autism. Happily there are others making the same journey that I have made. The search for more answers, the search for better results, must be our continuing reply to the frightened call for help that every autistic child makes when he behaves in his strange and seemingly alien manner.

SUGGESTED READING

These suggested readings are included for those parents who wish to obtain a more technical view of the subject of autism and of the present state of the work of others in this field.

Articles

Azima, H. and Cramer, F. J., "Effects of Partial Perceptual Isolation in Mentally Disturbed Individuals." *Dis. Nerv. Syst.* 17:117 (1956).

Benda, C.; Farrell, M.; and Chipman, C., "The Inadequacy of Present-Day Concepts of Mental Deficiency and Mental Illness of Child Psychiatry." *Amer. J. Psychiat.* 107:721 (1951).

Bergman, P. and Escalona, S., "Unusual Sensitivities in Very Young Children," in *Psychoanalytic Study of the Child,* Vols. III and IV (New York: International Universities Press, 1948).

Birch, H. G. and Leffard, A., "Intersensory Development in Children." *Monogr. Soc. Res. Child Develop.* 28:5 (1963).

Bruner, S. J., "The Cognitive Consequence of Early Sensory Deprivation." *Psychosom. Med.* 21:89–95 (1959).

Bryson, C., "Systematic Identification of Perceptual Disabilities in Autistic Children." *Percept. Motor Skills* 31:239 (1970).

Burlingham, D., "Occupations and Toys for Blind Children." *Int. J. Psychoanal.* 49:477 (1968).

Charney, I. W., "Regression and Reorganization in the 'Isolation Treatment' of Children: A Clinical Contribution to Sensory Deprivation Research." *J. Child Psych. & Psychiat.* 4:47 (1963).

Clancy, H. and Rendle-Short, J., "Infantile Autism—A Problem of Communication." *Aust. J. Occup. Therapy* 15(3) (1968).

Ferster, C. B., "Positive Reinforcement and Behavioral Deficits of Autistic Children." *Child Development* 32:437–56 (1961).

Frank, L. K., "Tactile Communication." *ECT* 16:31–80 (1958) and 56:209–55 (1957).

Freedman, A. M., "Treatment of Autistic Schizophrenic Children with Marsilid." *J. of Clin. & Exper. Psychopathology* XIX (1958), Suppl. 1, 138–45.

Fuller, J. L., "Experimental Deprivation and Later Behavior." *Science* 158:1642–46 (1967).

Gibbs, N., "Problems of Play and Mastery in the Blind Child." *Develop. Med. Child Neurol.* 11:516 (1969).

Gibby, R. G.; Adams, H. B.; and Carrera, R. N., "Therapeutic Changes in Psychiatric Patients Following Partial Sensory Deprivation (a Pilot Study)." *Arch. Gen. Psychiat.* 3:33 (1960).

Goldfarb, W. and Braunstein, P., "Reactions to Delayed Auditory Feedback Among a Group of Schizophrenic Children," in Hoch, P. H. and Zubin, J. (eds.), *Psychopathology of Communication* (New York: Grune & Stratton, 1958).

Goldfarb, W., "Receptor Preferences in Schizophrenic Children." *Arch. Neurol. Psychiat.* 76:643–52 (1956).

Grunberg, F. and Pond, D. A., "Conduct Disorders in Epileptic Children." *J. Neuro. Psychiat.* 20:65–68 (1957).

Hess, E., "Imprinting." *Science* 130:133–41 (1959).

Hewett, F. M., "Teaching Speech to an Autistic Child Through Operant Conditioning." *Amer. J. Orthopsychiat.* 35:927–36 (1965).

Ingram, R., "Chronic Brain Syndromes in Childhood Other than Cerebral Palsy, Epilepsy, and Mental Defect," in Bax, W. and MacKeith, R. (eds.), *Minimal Cerebral Dysfunction* (London: Heineman, 1963).

Kennard, M. and Levy, S., "The Meaning of Abnormal Electroencephalograms in Schizophrenia." *J. of Nerv. and Ment. Diseases* CXVI (1952), 413.

Levine, S.; Chevalier, J. A.; and Korchin, S. J., "The Effects of Shock and Handling in Infancy on Later Avoidance Learning." *J. Personality* 24:475–93 (1956).

Levine, S. and Lewis, G. W., "The Relative Importance of Experimenter Contact in an Effect Produced by Extra-stimulation in Infancy." *J. Comp. Physiol.* 52:368–69 (1959).

Menolascino, F. J., "Autistic Reactions in Early Childhood: Differential Diagnostic Consideration." *J. Child Psychol.* 6:203–18 (1965).

Metz, J. R., "Stimulation Level Preferences of Autistic Children." *J. Abnormal Psychology* 72:529–35 (1967).

Montague, M. F. A., "The Sensory Influences of the Skin." *Tex. Rep. Biol. Med.* 11:291–391 (1953).

O'Connor, N. and Hermelin, B., "Sensory Dominance." *Arch. Gen. Psych.* 12:99–103 (1965).

Papaz, J. W., "A Proposed Mechanism of Emotion." *Arch. Neurol. Psychiatry* 38:725–43 (1937).

Phillips, E. E., "Contributions to a Learning Theory Account of Childhood Autism." *J. Psychology* 43:117–25 (1957).

Pitfield, M. and Oppenheim, A. N., "Child Rearing Attitudes of Mothers of Psychotic Children." *J. Child Psychol. Psychiat.* 5:51 (1964).

Renshaw, S., "The Errors of Cutaneous Localization and the Effect of Practice on the Localizing Movement in Children and Adults." *J. Genetic Psychol.* 28:223–38 (1930).

Renshaw, S.; Wherry, R. J.; and Newlin, J. C., "Cutaneous Localization in Congenitally Blind Versus Seeing Children and Adults." *J. Genetic Psychol.* 28:239–48 (1930).

Rutter, M., "Concepts of Autism: A Review of Research." *J. Child Psychol. Psychiat.* 9:1 (1968).

——, "The Influence of Organic and Emotional Factors on the Origins, Nature and Outcome of Childhood Psychosis." *Develop. Med. Child Neurol.* 7:518 (1965).

Safrin, Renate Kersten, "Difference in Visual Perception and in Visual-Motor Functioning Between Psychotic and non-Psychotic Children." *J. of Consulting Psychology* XXVIII (1964), 41–46.

Schaeffer, H. R., and Emerson, P. E., "Patterns of Response to Physical Contact in Early Human Development." *J. Child Psychol. Psychiat.* 1:1–14 (1964).

Smolen, E. and Rosner, S., "Subclinical Organicity: A Problem in Diagnosis and Treatment." Presented at American Psychiatric Assoc. annual meeting, Chicago (1961).

Wieland, I. H. and Rudnick, R., "Considerations on the Development and Treatment of Autistic Childhood Psychosis." "The Psychoanalytic Study of the Child." 16:549–63 (1961).

——, "Development of Object Relationships and Childhood Psychosis." *J. Amer. Acad. Child. Psychiat.* 3:317–29 (1964).

Wing, J., "Diagnosis, Epidemiology, Aetiology," in Wing, J. K. (ed.), *Early Childhood Autism* (Oxford: Pergamon Press, 1966), pp. 3–49.

Books

Ayllion, T. and Azrin, N. H., *The Token Economy: A Motivational System for Therapy and Rehabilitation* (New York: Appleton-Century-Crofts, 1968).

Bekesy, G. V., *Sensory Inhibition* (Princeton, N.J.: Princeton University Press, 1967).

D'Ambrosio, R., *No Language but a Cry* (Garden City, N.Y.: Doubleday, 1970).

Gibson, J. J., *The Perception of the Visual World* (Boston: Houghton Mifflin, 1950).

Hock, P. H. and Zubin, J. (eds.), *Psychopathology of Communication* (New York: Grune & Stratton, 1958).

Myklebast, Helmer R., *Auditory Disorders in Children* (New York: Grune & Stratton, 1954).

Noback, C. R. and Montagna, W., *The Private Brain* (New York: Appleton-Century-Crofts, 1970).

O'Gorman, G., *The Nature of Childhood Autism* (New York: Appleton-Century-Crofts, 1967).

Sherrington, C. S., *The Integrative Action of the Nervous System* (London: Cambridge University Press, 1906).

Vygotsky, L. S., *Thought and Language* (Cambridge, Mass.: M.I.T. Press, 1962).

Woodburne, L. S., *The Neural Basis of Behavior* (Columbus, O.: Merrill, 1967).

BIBLIOGRAPHY

Ardrey, Robert, *African Genesis* (New York: Atheneum, 1961).

——, *The Territorial Imperative* (New York: Atheneum, 1966).

——, *The Social Contract* (New York: Atheneum, 1970).

Bender, L., "The Brain and Child Behavior." *Archives of General Psychiatry* 4:531 (1961).

——, "Autism in Children with Mental Deficiency." *American Journal of Mental Deficiency* 63:81–86 (1959).

——, "Schizophrenia in Childhood—Its Recognition, Description, and Treatment." *American Journal of Orthopsychiatry* 26:499–506 (1956).

Bergman, P. and Escalona, S., "Unusual Sensitivities in Very Young Children." *Psychoanalytical Studies of Children* 3–4:333–52 (1949).

Bettleheim, Bruno, *The Empty Fortress: Infantile Autism and the Birth of Self* (New York: The Free Press, 1967).

Blackwell, R. and Joynt, R., *Learning Disabilities Handbook for Teachers* (Springfield, Ill.: Charles C Thomas, 1972).

"Breaking Through to the Autistic Child." *Medical World News* (October 1966).

Call, J. D., "Newborn Approach Behavior and Early Ego Development." *International Journal of Psychoanalysis* 45:286–95 (1964).

Churchill, I.; Alpern, G.; and De Meyer, M., *Infantile Autism* (Springfield, Ill.: Charles C Thomas, 1971).

Clements, S.; Lehtinen, L.; and Lukens, J., *Children with Minimal Brain Injury* (Chicago: National Society for Crippled Children and Adults, 1963).

Dart, Raymond A., *Adventures with the Missing Link* (New York: The Viking Press, 1959).

Delacato, Carl H., *A New Start for the Child with Reading Problems: A Manual for Parents* (New York: David McKay, 1970).

——, *Neurological Organization and Reading* (Springfield, Ill.: Charles C Thomas, 1966).

——, *The Diagnosis and Treatment of Speech and Reading Problems* (Springfield, Ill.: Charles C Thomas, 1963).

——, *The Treatment and Prevention of Reading Problems* (Springfield, Ill.: Charles C Thomas, 1959).

Delacato, C. and Doman, G., "Hemiplegia and Concomitant Psychological Phenomenon." *American Journal of Occupational Therapy* X:4 (July–August, Part I, 1956).

Doman, Glenn J., *How to Teach Your Baby to Read* (New York: Random House, 1964).

——, *What to Do About Your Brain-injured Child* (Garden City, N.Y.: Doubleday, 1974).

Eisenberg, L. and Kanner, L., "Early Infantile Autism." *American Journal of Orthopsychiatry* 26:556–66 (1956).

"Electrical Helmet Strikes Back at Autism." *Medical World News* (January 1971).

Gunther, M., "Infant Behavior at the Breast," in E. M. Foss (ed.), *Determinants of Infant Behavior* (London: Methuen, 1961).

Kanner, L., "Problems of Nosology and Psycho Dynamics of Early Infantile Autism." *American Journal of Orthopsychiatry* 19:426 (1949).

——, "Autistic Disturbances of Affective Contact." *Nerv. Children* 2:217 (1943).

——, "General Concept of Schizophrenia at Different Ages." *Neurology and Psychiatry in Childhood* (Baltimore: Williams and Wilkins, 1954).

Klosovski, B. N., *The Development of the Brain and Its Disturbance by Harmful Factors* (New York: Macmillan, 1962).

Kohut, H., "Introspections, Empathy, and Psychoanalysis." *Journal of American Psychoanalytic Association* 7:459–87 (1959).

Kysar, J., "The Two Camps in Child Psychiatry: A Report from a Psychiatrist-Father of an Autistic and Retarded Child." *American Journal of Psychiatry* I(125):141–46 (July 1968).

Leek, Sybil, *Diary of a Witch* (New York: New American Library, 1969).

LeWinn, E. B., *Human Neurological Organization* (Springfield, Ill.: Charles C Thomas, 1968).

Lorenz, Konrad, *King Solomon's Ring* (New York: Thomas Y. Crowell, 1952).

——, *On Aggression* (New York: Harcourt, Brace & World, 1966).

Mair, Lucy, *Witchcraft* (New York: McGraw-Hill, 1969).

Melton, David, *When Children Need Help* (New York: Thomas Y. Crowell, 1972).

Morris, Desmond, *The Naked Ape* (New York: McGraw-Hill, 1967).

——, *The Human Zoo* (New York: McGraw-Hill, 1969).

——, *Intimate Behavior* (New York: McGraw-Hill, 1972).

Murray, Margaret A., *The God of the Witches* (New York: Oxford University Press, 1931, 1970).

——, *The Witch-Cult in Western Europe* (Oxford: Clarendon Press, 1921, 1971).

Ornitz, E., "Disorders of Perception Common to Early Infantile Autism and Schizophrenia." *Comp. Psychiatry* 10(4):259 (1969).

Ornitz, E. and Ritvo, E., "Perceptual Inconstancy of Early Autism." *Archives of General Psychiatry* 18:76–98 (1968).

——, "Neurophysiologic Mechanisms Underlying Perceptual Inconstancy in Autistic and Schizophrenic Children." *Archives of General Psychiatry* 19:22 (1968).

"Parents as Scapegoats." *Human Behavior* 1(3):8.

Piaget, J., *The Construction of Reality in a Child* (New York: Basic Books, 1954).

——, *The Origins of Intelligence in Children* (New York: International Universities Press, 1952).

Reisen, A. H., "Effects of Stimulus Deprivation on the Development of Atrophy of the Visual Sensory System." *American Journal of Orthoptics* 30:23–26 (1960).

Rimland, B., *Infantile Autism: The Syndrome and Its Implication for a Neural Theory of Behavior* (New York: Appleton-Century-Crofts, 1964).

——, "The Effect of High Dosage Levels of Certain Vitamins on the Behavior of Children with Severe Mental Disorders," in Hawkins, D. R. and Pauling, L. (eds.), *Orthomolecular Psychiatry* (San Francisco: W. H. Freeman, 1971).

Ritvo, E.; Ornitz, E.; and La Franchi, S., "Frequency of Repetitive Behaviors in Early Infantile Autism and Its Variants." *Archives of General Psychiatry* 19:341 (1968).

Ritvos, S. and Provence, S., "Form Perception and Imitation in Some Autistic Children: Diagnostic Findings and Their Contextual Interpretation." *Psychoanal. Stud. Child.* 8:115–61 (1953).

Roboth, Frances Diane, *Chronicles of Old Salem* (New York: Bonanza Books, 1948).

Rosenzweig, M. R.; Krech, D.; Bennett, E. L.; and Damond, M. C., "Effects of Environmental Complexity and Training on Brain Chemistry and Anatomy: A Replication and Extension." *Journal Comp. Physiol. Psychol.* 55:429–37 (1962).

Schopler, E., "Early Infantile Autism and the Receptor Processes." *Archives of General Psychiatry* 13:327–37 (1965).

——, "Visual Versus Tactual Receptor Preferences in Normal and Schizophrenic Children." *Journal of Abnormal Psychology* 71:108–14 (1966).

Shevrin, H. and Toussieng, P., "Conflict over Tactile Experience in Emotionally Disturbed Children." *Journal of American Academy of Child Psychiatry* 1:564–90 (1962).

Summers, Montagne, *The History of Witchcraft* (New Hyde Park, New York: University Books, 1956).

Thomas, Evan W., *Brain-Injured Children* (Springfield, Ill.: Charles C Thomas, 1969).

Tindall, G., *A Handbook on Witches* (New York: Atheneum, 1966).

Wolf, James, *The Results of Treatment of Cerebral Palsy* (Springfield, Ill.: Charles C Thomas, 1969).

INDEX